METROPOLITAN FASHIONS
OF THE 1880s

FROM THE 1885 BUTTERICK CATALOG

Butterick Publishing Co.

DOVER PUBLICATIONS, INC.
Mineola, New York

Copyright

Copyright © 1997 by Dover Publications, Inc.
All rights reserved under Pan American and International Copyright Conventions.

Published in Canada by General Publishing Company, Ltd., 30 Lesmill Road, Don Mills, Toronto, Ontario.
Published in the United Kingdom by Constable and Company, Ltd., 3 The Lanchesters, 162–164 Fulham Palace Road, London W6 9ER.

Bibliographical Note

This Dover edition, first published in 1997, is a new selection of material from *Metropolitan Fashions for Spring and Summer, 1885, Vol. XXI, No. 1*, published by The Butterick Publishing Co. (Limited), London and New York, n.d. [1885]. A new Introduction has been written for this edition.

Library of Congress Cataloging-in-Publication Data

Metropolitan fashions of the 1880s : from the 1885 Butterick catalog / Butterick Publishing Co.
   p.   cm.
   Selection of material from Metropolitan fashons for spring and summer 1885, vol. XXI, no. 1, published by the Butterick Pub. Co., London and New York, 1885. With a new introd.
  ISBN 0-486-29706-3 (pbk.)
   1. Dressmaking—Patterns—Catalogs. 2. Tailoring—Pattens—Catalogs. 3. Costume—United States—History—19th century.
I. Butterick Publishing Company.
TT520.M46 1997
746.9'2'097309041—dc21   97-13138
                                              CIP

Manufactured in the United States of America
Dover Publications, Inc., 31 East 2nd Street, Mineola, N.Y. 11501

INTRODUCTION

BEFORE THE ADVENT of ready-to-wear—quite a recent development on the fashion scene—most clothing was custom-made. While the well-to-do had their clothes made by a tailor or dressmaker, most people's clothing was made at home by the women of the family. In 1846, an American, Elias Howe, applied for and received a patent on a sewing machine, allowing a seamstress to put seams together quickly. However, to determine how to cut and assemble a garment, the seamstress had to depend, for the most part, upon older garments or her own pattern-drafting skills. As clothing grew more and more elaborate, producing a well-fitting, fashionable garment became more and more of a challenge.

Many fashion periodicals featured small-scale pattern drawings that had to be enlarged; a few even featured full-size patterns, but these were for one size only and had to be adapted for the individual wearer. By the 1860s, it was even possible to purchase, through the fashion magazines, a pattern custom-made to one's own measurements. In 1863, Ebenezer Butterick, a tailor, and his wife, introduced the paper pattern with graded sizes. The first patterns were for boy's shirts, but women's and children's patterns, added to the line in 1866, very quickly made up the majority of the designs. The Buttericks' success was overwhelming—the Buttericks sold over 6,000,000 patterns in 1871, despite the fact that other companies had begun to manufacture patterns as well.

In order to publicize his patterns, twice a year Butterick published a catalog, *Metropolitan Fashions,* showing their current fashions and featuring new patterns. The present volume is a selection of new fashions from the spring/summer 1885 issue, together with the original captions. *Metropolitan Fashions* was directed to the middle-class woman with a family. Everyday clothes for women predominate—only two garments, the "ladies' trained costume" and the "ladies' pointed basque" on page 42, are obvi-ously intended for evening. On page 41 is shown a "ladies' mourning toilette," combining a skirt and basque pattern also shown individually. Besides dresses, skirts, basques, coats and other wraps, there are also patterns for ladies' chemises and corset covers, wrappers (including one made from a blanket, page 56) and even a ladies' negligée (page 89). Approximately one third of the patterns shown are for children. Men, however, are sadly neglected; only two patterns for gentlemen are included in the book (pages 9 and 10). Also included are patterns for accessories such as collars, mittens, fichus, stockings, tam-o'-shanter caps and aprons, as well as patterns for dolls and costumes for dolls.

Many of the fashions in the catalog were shown more than once, often on widely separated pages, in order to show variations in fabric and trim. The original captions, therefore, contain cross references to other pages. In the present volume, all variations of a single pattern are grouped on the same or on facing pages, so these cross references should be ignored.

The most striking feature of the fashions in this volume is, of course, the bustle. First popularized in the early 1870s, the bustle had begun to disappear towards the end of that decade. By 1885, however, it was back, more exaggerated than ever. Skirts were often draped in the front, with the extra fullness pulled around to the back and draped over the bustle. In contrast, the bodice was quite sleek, with a princess-line basque, a high neckline and smoothly fitted sleeves with very little fullness in the cap. Given the use of heavy fabrics, the elaborate draping of skirts and the abundance of braids, scallops and other trimmings, women appeared to be, not so much dressed, as upholstered.

Metropolitan Fashions of the 1880s offers an in-depth look at the everyday fashions of a period that featured one of the most bizarre silhouettes in fashion history.

NO. 9560.—LADIES' BASQUE.—This stylish garment is here illustrated as made of plain dress goods, with machine-stitching and fancy buttons for a finish. The pattern is in 13 sizes for ladies from 28 to 46 inches, bust measure. To make the garment for a lady of medium size, will require 3⅞ yards of material 22 inches wide, or 1¾ yard of goods 48 inches wide. Price of pattern, 1s. or 25 cents.

9560

9560

9566

No. 9566.—LADIES' DOUBLE-BREASTED COAT.—This jaunty pattern is in 13 sizes for ladies from 28 to 46 inches, bust measure, and will develop satisfactorily in any coating fabric at present in vogue. Braids, bands or *passementerie* ornaments may be applied to the edges of such coats, and the collar and lapels, and also the wrists of the sleeves, may be faced with velvet, plush or other decorative goods. To make the garment for a lady of medium size, will require 4⅝ yards of material 22 inches wide, or 2⅛ yards of goods 48 inches wide. Price of pattern, 1s. 3d. or 30 cents.

9566

FIGURE NO. 266.—LADIES' COSTUME.—This illustrates Ladies' costume No. 9558, two views of which are given on page 61.* It is here made of striped *frisé* dress goods, with the same and Titan braid for trimming. It unites a round walking-skirt with an effective front-drapery permanently attached, and a well-fitting over-dress with basque front and polonaise back. The pattern is in 13 sizes for ladies from 28 to 46 inches, bust measure. For a lady of medium size, it needs 11¼ yards of material 22 inches wide, or 6 yards 48 inches wide. Price of pattern, 1s. 6d. or 35 cents.

9558

9558

No. 9558.—LADIES' COSTUME.—Another illustration of this stylish costume may be observed at figure No. 266 on page 64, where it is shown in a different material, with other trimmings. Checked goods of a pretty shade are represented in the present instance, and the scolloped edges are bound with satin. The skirt is trimmed with three narrow plaitings, the upper one being set on to form its own heading. The pattern is in 13 sizes for ladies from 28 to 46 inches, bust measure. For a lady of medium size, it needs 11¼ yards of goods 22 inches wide, or 6 yards 48 inches wide. Price of pattern, 1s. 6d. or 35 cents.

*Page references should be ignored throughout. In this edition, all views of a pattern are on the same page or on facing pages.

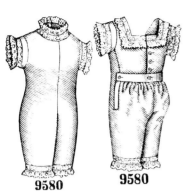

9580   **9580**

No. 9580.—Child's Under-Waist and Drawers.—This pattern is in 9 sizes for children from 2 to 10 years of age, and may be employed for any material adapted to the construction of garments intended for underwear. To make the garment for a child of 6 years, will require 2 yards of material 27 inches wide. If material 36 inches wide be selected, then 1⅝ yard will suffice. Price of pattern, 10d. or 20 cents.

9569

No. 9569.—Ladies' Wrapper.—Flowered woolen goods were employed for this wrapper, and ties of satin ribbon are arranged in a handsome bow over the closing. The lower edge of the skirt portion is completed with two rows of fine plaiting, the upper row being sewed on to form its own heading. The pattern is in 13 sizes for ladies from 28 to 46 inches, bust measure. To make the garment for a lady of medium size, will require 9⅝ yards of material 22 inches wide, or 7 yards 36 inches wide, or 4½ yards 48 inches wide. Price of pattern, 1s. 6d. or 35 cents.

9569

Figure No. 267.—Child's Cloak.—This illustrates Child's cloak No. 9557, which is also shown on page 60. Plain velvet and fancy cloaking of a seasonable variety are united in the present instance, with buttons for trimming. The pattern is in 5 sizes for children from 2 to 6 years of age, and costs 10d. or 20 cents. Any seasonable variety of cloaking material may be chosen for its construction, and any simple trimming may be added with good effect. To make the cloak for a child of 6 years, will require 3¾ yards of material 22 inches wide, or 3⅜ yards 27 inches wide, or 1⅜ yard 48 inches wide.

9557

No. 9557.—Child's Cloak.—This pattern, again shown at figure No. 267 on page 64, is in 5 sizes for children from 2 to 6 years of age, and may be used for any cloaking fabric, with any suitable decoration. To make the garment for a child of 6 years, will require 3⅞ yards of material 22 inches wide, or 1⅞ yard 48 inches wide. Price of pattern, 10d. or 20 cents.

9557

9571

No. 9571.—Ladies' Apron.—This apron is made of figured and plain wash goods in the present instance, with narrow embroidery for trimming. If preferred, one variety of material may be employed throughout, and any different decoration the taste of the maker may suggest may be selected instead of that here pictured. The pattern is in one size, and, for an apron like it, requires 1½ yard of figured material and ⅜ yard of plain goods, each 22 inches wide. Price of pattern, 7d. or 15 cents.

No. 9556.—Ladies' Coat.—Striped cloth of a Winter texture was employed for this jaunty coat, with buttons for trimming. The pattern is in 13 sizes for ladies from 28 to 46 inches, bust measure. To make the garment for a lady of medium size, will require 4 yards of material 22 inches wide, or 1⅞ yard 48 inches wide. If 54-inch-wide goods be selected, then 1⅝ yard will suffice. Price of pattern, 1s. 3d. or 30 cents.

9556   **9556**

9587   9587

No. 9587.—LADIES'
FRENCH SLEEVE. — This
pattern is in 3 sizes—11,
13 and 15 inches, measur-
ing around the muscular
part of the upper arm. To
make a pair of sleeves for
a lady whose arm meas-
ures 13 inches as mentioned,
needs 1¼ yard of goods 22
inches wide, or ⅝ yard 48
inches wide. Price of
pattern, 5d. or 10 cents.

9588

No. 9588.—MITTEN PATTERN.—Cashmere, cloth, chamois
and other goods suitable for the purpose may be made up by
this convenient pattern, which is in 5 sizes from 5 to 9 inches, measuring the hand just back of the knuckles. A pair of
mittens for a lady whose hand measures 7 inches, requires 1⅛
yard of goods 24 inches wide. Price of pattern, 5d. or 10 cents.

No. 9564.—GIRLS'
APRON.—Fine nain-
sook was selected
for this apron, and
embroidered edging
provides the garni-
ture. The pattern
is in 8 sizes for girls
from 2 to 9 years
of age, and may be
used for any mate-
rial suitable for
aprons. To make
the apron for a girl
of 8 years, requires
1¼ yard of goods
36 inches wide.
Price of pattern,
7d. or 15 cents.

9564   9564

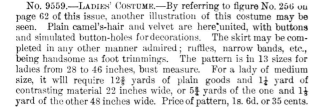

9559   9559

No. 9559.—LADIES' COSTUME.—By referring to figure No. 256 on
page 62 of this issue, another illustration of this costume may be
seen. Plain camel's-hair and velvet are here united, with buttons
and simulated button-holes for decorations. The skirt may be completed in any other manner admired; ruffles, narrow bands, etc.,
being handsome as foot trimmings. The pattern is in 13 sizes for
ladies from 28 to 46 inches, bust measure. For a lady of medium
size, it will require 12⅝ yards of plain goods and 1¼ yard of
contrasting material 22 inches wide, or 5¾ yards of the one and 1⅛
yard of the other 48 inches wide. Price of pattern, 1s. 6d. or 35 cents.

FIGURE NO. 256.—LADIES' COSTUME.—This illustrates Ladies' costume No. 9559,
which is represented in a different combination of goods and trimmings on page
61 of this issue. The materials employed for it in this instance are brocaded and
plain velvet and satin-finished silk, the garnitures combining the plain velvet and
silk and including satin cord and *passementerie* ornaments of cut jet. The com-
ponent parts of the costume are a basque body and an effectively draped walking-
skirt. Any preferred disposal of decorations may be followed, the jetted front-
gores now so fashionable being especially worthy of mention. The pattern is in
13 sizes for ladies from 28 to 46 inches, bust measure, and costs 1s. 6d. or 35
cents. To make the costume for a lady of medium size, requires 13⅜ yards of goods
22 inches wide, or 6⅞ yards 48 inches wide. Price of pattern, 1s. 6d. or 35 cents.

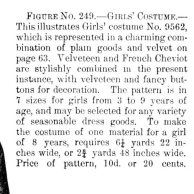

FIGURE NO. 249.—GIRLS' COSTUME.—This illustrates Girls' costume No. 9562, which is represented in a charming combination of plain goods and velvet on page 63. Velveteen and French Cheviot are stylishly combined in the present instance, with velveteen and fancy buttons for decoration. The pattern is in 7 sizes for girls from 3 to 9 years of age, and may be selected for any variety of seasonable dress goods. To make the costume of one material for a girl of 8 years, requires 6¼ yards 22 inches wide, or 2⅜ yards 48 inches wide. Price of pattern, 10d. or 20 cents.

No. 9562.—GIRLS' COSTUME.—This costume is pictured in another combination of materials at figure No. 249 on page 60 of this issue. The pattern is in 7 sizes for girls from 3 to 9 years of age. To make the garment for a girl of 8 years, requires 6¼ yards of material 22 inches wide, or 2⅜ yards of goods 48 inches wide. Price of pattern, 10d. or 20 cents.

9562   **9562**

No. 9593.—GIRLS' CLOAK.—Gray cloth and velvet were used for the cloak here represented, and a handsome cord-ornament decorates the back. The pattern is in 8 sizes for girls from 5 to 12 years of age. To make the garment for a girl of 8 years, will require 3¾ yards of goods 22 inches wide, or 1¾ yard of material 48 inches wide. Price of pattern, 1s. or 25 cents.

9593

9593

FIGURE NO. 262.—LADIES' HOUSE DRESS.—This illustrates Ladies' house dress No. 9561, again shown on page 62. It is here made of flowered cashmere and plain velvet, Surah being introduced in the decoration. Loops and ends of ribbon heighten its decorative effect, and lace ruffs are worn in the neck and wrists. If desired, a single variety of material may be employed, with tasteful results. The pattern is in 13 sizes for ladies from 28 to 46 inches, bust measure. Of one material for a lady of medium size, it will require 11½ yards 22 inches wide, or 5½ yards 48 inches wide. To make it as shown on page 62, requires 10¾ yards of brocaded goods 22 inches wide, with 1 yard of plain silk and 1⅛ yard of plain velvet, each 20 inches wide. Price of pattern, 1s. 6d. or 35 cents.

No. 9579.—Misses' Coat.—All kinds of coatings may be made up into garments of this description and the finish may be varied in any way to suit the taste. The pattern is in 8 sizes for misses from 8 to 15 years of age. To make the coat for a miss of 13 years, will require 3⅞ yards of material 22 inches wide, or 1⅞ yard 48 inches wide. Price of pattern, 1s. or 25 cents.

9579

9579

9570

9570

No. 9570.—Ladies' Fichu.—Fancy nets, gauzes, embroidered mulls, jetted Brussels, nets, silks, satins, etc., are appropriate for the formation of dressy adjuncts of this kind. Satin is employed for the garment in the present instance, and lace of a superior quality is employed for trimming. The pattern is in one size, and, for a fichu like it, needs ⅞ yard of goods 22 inches wide. Price of pattern, 5d. or 10 cents.

No. 9563.—Girls' Costume.—This pattern is again shown at figure No. 255 on page 62 of this issue. It is in 8 sizes for girls from 5 to 12 years of age. To make the costume for a girl of 8 years, needs 5⅝ yards of goods 22 inches wide, or 2⅜ yards 48 inches wide. Price of pattern, 1s. or 25 cents.

9563

9563

9561

9561

No. 9561.—Ladies' House Dress.—Another view of this garment may be observed at figure No. 262 on page 63 of this issue. Three materials—velvet, Surah and brocaded cashmere—were employed in its development in the present instance. The Surah is used for the vest portion, while the remainder is of the cashmere, with accessories of the velvet. This pattern is in 13 sizes for ladies from 28 to 46 inches, bust measure. For a lady of medium size, it will require 10¾ yards of brocaded goods 22 inches wide, with 1 yard of plain silk and 1⅜ yard of plain velvet, each 20 inches wide. Price of pattern, 1s. 6d. or 35 cents.

Figure No. 255.—Girls' Costume.—This illustrates Girls' costume No. 9563, which is differently pictured on page 64 of the present issue. Fancy suiting was employed for it in this instance. The pattern is in 8 sizes for girls from 5 to 12 years of age, and costs 1s. or 25 cents. To make the costume for a girl of 8 years, will require 5⅝ yards of material 22 inches wide, or 2¾ yards of goods 48 inches wide.

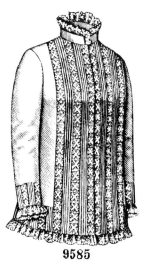

No. 9585.—LADIES' SHORT SACK NIGHT-WRAPPER.—This night-wrapper is made of cambric, with lace tucking and lace edging for trimming. The pattern is in 10 sizes for ladies from 28 to 46 inches, bust measure, and may be used for muslin, linen or any similar wash goods, with embroidery, tucks or any decoration admired by the maker. To make the garment for a lady of medium size, requires 2⅜ yards of material 36 inches wide, with 1⅝ yard of lace tucking 20 inches wide. Price of pattern, 10d. or 20 cents.

9585

No. 9589.—BOYS' BLOUSE-WAIST.—This stylish little pattern is in 8 sizes for boys from 5 to 12 years of age, and may be chosen for any variety of goods in vogue, with any tasteful trimming. To make the waist for a boy of 7 years, will require 2 yards of goods 27 inches wide. Price of pattern, 10d. or 20 cents.

9589   **9589**

No. 9565.—LADIES' BASQUE.—This basque is pictured in another material at figure No. 254 on page 62 of this issue. The pattern is in 13 sizes for ladies from 28 to 46 inches, bust measure. To make the garment for a lady of medium size, will require 2½ yards of goods 22 inches wide, or 1¼ yard 48 inches wide. Price of pattern, 1s. or 25 cents.

9565   **9565**

9582   **9582**

No. 9582.—LADIES' WALKING SKIRT.—Cloth, cassimere or any variety of fashionable dress goods may be made up in this pretty style, and ruffles, flounces, bands of fur or plush, braids or other decorations may take the place of the trimming pictured. The pattern is in 9 sizes for ladies from 20 to 36 inches, waist measure. To make the garment for a lady of medium size, will require 10¼ yards of goods 22 inches wide, or 5¼ yards 48 inches wide. Price of pattern, 1s. 3d. or 30 cents.

FIGURE No. 254.—LADIES' TOILETTE.—This consists of Ladies' basque No. 9565, again shown on page 61; and skirt No. 9537, also represented on page 27. The basque pattern is in 13 sizes for ladies from 28 to 46 inches, bust measure, and costs 1s. or 25 cents. The skirt pattern is in 9 sizes for ladies from 20 to 36 inches, waist measure, and costs 1s. or 25 cents. The toilette is here made of dark green velveteen, and the only decoration is a belt of ribbon draped in a knot with long loops and ends over the closing. To make the toilette for a lady of medium size, will require 12⅞ yards of material 28 inches wide: the basque needing 2½ yards; and the skirt, 10⅜ yards. If goods 48 inches wide be chosen, then 5⅞ yards will be sufficient: the basque needing 1¼ yard: and the skirt, 4⅝ yards.

No. 9573.—Child's Coat.—Another view of this coat, showing other material, with different trimming, is given at figure No. 259 on page 63. The pattern is in 6 sizes for children from 1 to 6 years of age. For a child of 6 years, it will need 3⅛ yards of goods 22 inches wide, or 2⅝ yards 27 inches wide, or 1½ yard 48 inches wide. Price of pattern, 7d. or 15 cts.

9573

9573

No. 9574.—Child's Costume.—This pattern, also shown at figure No. 265 on page 64, is in 6 sizes for children from 1 to 6 years of age. To make the costume for a child of 6 years, needs 3⅛ yards of material and ⅞ yard of contrasting goods 22 inches wide, or 1½ yard of the one and ½ yard of the other 48 inches wide. Price of pattern, 7d. or 15 cts.

9574   **9574**

FIGURE NO. 253.—MISSES' COSTUME.—This illustrates Misses' costume No. 9567, which is shown in other material on page 62 of this issue. Fine flannel suiting is the fabric used for it in the present instance, and the trimming consists of buttons, machine-stitching and a Jersey sash of scarlet Surah. The pattern is in 8 sizes for misses from 8 to 15 years of age. To make the costume for a miss of 13 years, will require 6¾ yards of material 22 inches wide, or 3½ yards of goods 48 inches wide. Price of pattern, 1s. 3d. or 30 cents.

FIGURE NO. 259.—CHILD'S COAT.—This illustrates Child's coat No. 9573, which is represented in two views on page 60 of the present issue. The pattern is in 6 sizes for children from 1 to 6 years of age. To make the garment for a child of 6 years, will require 3⅛ yards of material 22 inches wide, or 2⅝ yards 27 inches wide, or 1½ yard 48 inches wide. Price of pattern, 7d. or 15 cents.

FIGURE NO. 265.—CHILD'S COSTUME.—This illustrates Child's costume No. 9574, which is differently represented in two views on page 60 of this publication. The pattern is in 6 sizes for children from 1 to 6 years of age. To make the costume for a child of 6 years, will require 3⅛ yards of one material and ⅞ yard of contrasting goods, each 22 inches wide. Price of pattern, 7d. or 15 cents.

No. 9567.—Misses' Costume.—Another view of this costume, showing different material and a Jersey sash, may be seen at figure No. 253 on page 61. Dark blue flannel was employed for it in this instance, and buttons comprise the only trimmings. The pattern is in 8 sizes for misses from 8 to 15 years of age. To make the costume for a miss of 13 years, requires 6¾ yards of material 22 inches wide, or 3½ yards of goods 48 inches wide. Price of pattern, 1s. 3d. or 30 cents.

9567   **9567**

9577

No. 9577.—
Child's Cloak.—
This pattern, again
shown at figure No.
258 on page 63, is in
7 sizes for children
from 6 months to
6 years of age.
For a child of 6
years, it requires 3½
yards of material 22
inches wide, or 2⅞
yards 27 inches
wide, or 2 yards
48 inches wide.
Price of pattern,
10d. or 20 cents.

9577

9581

No. 9581.—La-
dies' Wrap.—
Fancy-figured
cloth was em-
ployed in the for-
mation of the hand-
some wrap here
represented, and
fringe provides the
trimming. All
kinds of wrap
goods may be
made up in this
way, and chenille,
plush or velvet
bands, braids,
laces or other
garnitures may be
applied to the
edges, with becom-
ing results. The
pattern is in 10
sizes for ladies
from 28 to 46 in-

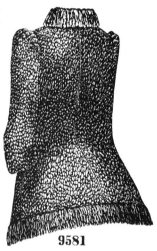

9581

ches, bust measure. To make the garment for a lady
of medium size, requires 3¾ yards of goods 22 inches
wide, or 1⅞ yard 48 inches wide, or 1⅞ yard 54
inches wide. Price of pattern, 1s. 3d. or 30 cents.

FIGURE NO. 258.—CHILD'S STREET SUIT.
—This consists of Child's cloak No. 9577,
shown on page 60; and Girls' cap No. 9576,
shown on page 64. The cloak pattern is in 7
sizes for children from 6 months to 6 years
old, and costs 10d. or 20 cents. The cap
pattern is in 5 sizes for girls from 1 to 9
years old, and costs 5d. or 10 cents. For a
child of 6 years, the cloak needs 3½ yards
of goods, and the cap ¾ yard, each 22 inches wide, with ½ yard of silk for cap lining.

No. 9572.—
Misses' Dress.—
This dress is
pictured in other
material, with
other trimming,
at figure No. 257
on page 63 of
the present issue.
The pattern
is in 8 sizes for
misses from 8 to
15 years of age.
Of one material for
a miss of 13 years,
it will require 6⅓
yards 22 inches
wide, or 3 yards
48 inches wide.
As illustrated, it
calls for 5 yards
of goods 22 inches
wide, together
with 2⅓ yards of
silk 20 inches
wide for the collar
and scarf-ties.
Price of pattern,
1s. 3d. or 30 cents.

9572

9572

FIGURE NO. 257.—MISSES' DRESS.—This illustrates Misses' dress
No. 9572, which is differently represented on page 62 of this issue.
The pattern is in 8 sizes for misses from 8 to 15 years of age, and
may be used for any dress goods in vogue, with any pretty decoration.
To make the dress for a miss of 13 years, will require 5 yards of
goods 22 inches wide, with 2⅓ yards of silk 20 inches wide for the
collar and scarf-ties. Of one material, it needs 6⅓ yards 22 inches
wide, or 3 yards 48 inches wide. Price of pattern, 1s. 3d. or 30 cents.

No. 9598.—
GENTLEMEN'S
KNICKERBOCKERS.
—Mixed cloth was
selected for the
garment here re-
presented. The
pattern is in 7
sizes for gentle-
men from 28 to
40 inches, waist
measure. To make
the Knickerbock-
ers for a gentleman
of 32 inches, waist
measure, requires
2¼ yards of goods
27 inches wide.
Price of pattern,
1s. or 25 cents.

9598   **9598**

No. 9568.—LA-
DIES' WAIST, WITH
PEASANT BODICE.
—At figure No.
252 on page 61,
this waist is also
shown. The pat-
tern is in 13 sizes
for ladies from 28
to 46 inches, bust
measure. For a
lady of medium
size, it needs 1¾
yard of velvet 20
inches wide, with
⅞ yard of lining 36
inches wide, and
1⅞ yard of lace net
27 inches wide.
Price, 1s. or 25 cts.

9568   **9568**

9578   **9578**

No. 9578.—LADIES' OVER-SKIRT.—This over-skirt is also pictured at
figure No. 252 elsewhere on this page. Serge suiting was the material employed for it in the present instance, with braid for decoration.
The pattern is in 9 sizes for ladies from 20 to 36 inches, waist measure, and may be used for any dress goods
in vogue. To make the garment for a lady
of medium size, will require 5¼ yards of
material 22 inches wide, or 2⅝ yards 48 inches wide. Price of pattern, 1s. or 25 cents.

9594   **9594**

No. 9594.—INFANTS' CIRCULAR CLOAK.—White cashmere was used for the cloak pictured in these engravings, with oriental lace for trimming. Piqué, Marseilles
or any material employed for such garments may be
made up in this way. The pattern is in one size, and, to
make a garment like it, will require 3¾ yards of goods
22 inches wide, or 3¼ yards 27 inches wide, or 1⅝ yard
48 inches wide. Price of pattern, 10d. or 20 cents.

FIGURE NO. 252.—LADIES' TOILETTE.—This illustrates Ladies' waist No. 9568, differently portrayed on page 64; over-skirt No. 9578, again pictured on this page; and skirt No.
8682, shown on page 28. The waist pattern is in 13 sizes for ladies from 28 to 46 inches, bust
measure, and costs 1s. or 25 cents. The patterns to the skirt and over-skirt are each in 9 sizes
for ladies from 20 to 36 inches, waist measure: the over-skirt costing 1s. or 25 cents; and the
skirt, 1s. 3d. or 30 cents. Of one material for a lady of medium size, they need 14¼ yards 22
inches wide: the waist requiring 4⅘ yards; the over-skirt, 5¼ yards; and the skirt, 4½ yards.

No. 9583.—GIRLS' CLOAK.—This pretty little cloak is again shown at figure No. 250 on page 60 of this publication. The pattern is in 7 sizes for girls from 3 to 9 years of age. To make the cloak for a girl of 8 years, will require 3⅛ yards of goods 22 inches wide, or 1⅜ yard of material 48 inches wide. Price of pattern, 10d. or 20 cents.

9583

9583

9597

No. 9597.—GENTLEMEN'S JACKET.—This pattern is in 7 sizes for gentlemen from 32 to 44 inches, breast measure. To make the jacket for a gentleman of 36 inches, breast measure, needs 4 yards of goods 27 inches wide, or 2 yards of material 54 inches wide. Price of pattern, 1s. 3d. or 30 cents.

9597

FIGURE NO. 250.—GIRLS' CLOAK.—This illustrates Girls' cloak No. 9583, which is again shown on page 63 of this issue. Fancy cloth is the material used for it in the present instance, with velvet and buttons for trimming. The pattern is in 7 sizes for girls from 3 to 9 years of age, and is adapted to all varieties of cloaking in vogue. To make the garment of one material for a girl of 8 years, will require 3⅞ yards 22 inches wide, or 3 yards 27 inches wide, or 1¾ yard 48 inches wide. Price of pattern, 10d. or 20 cents.

No. 9584.—MISSES' COAT.—This coat is shown in other material at figure No. 251 on page 61. Fancy coating was employed for its construction in this instance. The pattern is in 8 sizes for misses from 8 to 15 years of age. To make the coat for a miss of 13 years, will require 3¼ yards of material 22 inches wide, or 1¾ yard of goods 48 inches wide. Price of pattern, 1s. or 25 cents.

9584

9575

No. 9575.—LADIES' AND MISSES' TAM O'SHANTER CAP.—This cap is again shown at figure No. 251 on page 61. The pattern is in 6 sizes from 20½ to 23 inches, head measures. For a person whose head measures 22 inches, it needs 1¼ yard of goods 22 inches wide, or ⅞ yard 48 inches wide, each with 1¼ yard of silk 20 inches wide to line. Price of pattern, 7d. or 15 cents.

FIGURE NO. 251.—MISSES' STREET TOILETTE.—This consists of Misses' skirt No. 9586, illustrated on page 64 of this issue; coat No. 9584, also shown on page 63; and cap No. 9575, shown on page 64. The coat and skirt patterns are each in 8 sizes for misses from 8 to 15 years of age, and each costs 1s. or 25 cents. The cap pattern is in 6 sizes from 20½ to 23 inches, head measures, and costs 7d. or 15 cents. To make the costume for a miss of 13 years, needs 11⅝ yards of material 22 inches wide; the coat calling for 3¼ yards, the skirt for 7 yards, and the cap for 1⅜ yard.

9584

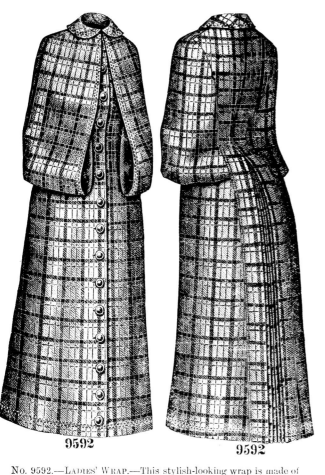

9592   **9592**

No. 9590.—
Misses' Costume.
—Another view of
this stylish cos-
tume may be ob-
served at figure
No. 260 on page
63. The pattern
is in 8 sizes for
misses from 8 to
15 years of age,
and, while par-
ticularly favored
for light-weight
cloths and similar
fabrics, is also
adapted to any
dress goods now
in vogue. To
make the costume
for a miss of 13
years, will require
9½ yards of ma-
terial 22 inches
wide, or 4½ yards
48 inches wide.
Price of pattern,
1s. 3d. or 30 cents.

9590   **9590**

No. 9592.—Ladies' Wrap.—This stylish-looking wrap is made of mode-and-brown plaid cloth, with machine-stitching as the decoration. The pattern is in 10 sizes for ladies from 28 to 46 inches, bust measure, and may be selected for any wrap fabric in vogue. If a more elaborate finish be desired, bands of plush or velvet may be applied to the edges. To make the garment for a lady of medium size, will require 8 yards of material 22 inches wide, or 4 yards 48 inches wide, or 3⅝ yards 54 inches wide. Price of pattern, 1s. 6d. or 35 cents.

No. 9591.—
Ladies' Dress.
—The stylishly
devised dress
pictured in
these engrav-
ings is made
of dark gray
suiting, with
bands and fac-
ings of velvet
for decoration.
The pattern is
in 13 sizes for
ladies from 28
to 46 inches,
bust measure,
and may be
employed for
cashmere,
camel's-hair,
serge and all
other varieties
of dress goods
at present in
vogue, with
any trimming
that may be
desired by the
maker. To
make the dress
for a lady of
medium size,
will require 7⅝
yards of ma-
terial 22 inch-
es wide, or 3¼
yards 48 inch-
es wide. Price
of pattern, 1s.
6d. or 35 cents.

9591

9591

FIGURE No. 260.—Misses' Costume.—This illustrates Misses' costume No. 9590, which is represented in a single variety of material, with a different method of completion, on page 62 of the present issue. The pattern is in 8 sizes for misses from 8 to 15 years of age, and is adapted to all sorts of seasonable dress goods, whether alone or in combination. To make the costume of one material for a miss of 13 years, needs 9½ yards 22 inches wide. If goods 48 inches wide be chosen, then 4½ yards will be sufficient for the purpose. Price of pattern, 1s. 3d. or 30 cents.

FIGURE NO. 281.—MISSES' TOILETTE.—This consists of Misses' basque No. 9599, and skirt No. 9600, both of which are also represented on page 67 of this issue. The toilette is here made of cloth, with trimmings of the same, braid, machine-stitching and ribbon. The patterns are each in 8 sizes for misses from 8 to 15 years of age: the basque costing 10d. or 20 cents; and the skirt, 1s. or 25 cents. To make the toilette for a miss of 13 years, will require 9¾ yards of material 22 inches wide: the skirt needing 6⅝ yards; and the basque, 3¼ yards. Of 48-inch-wide goods, 5 yards will suffice: the skirt requiring 3½ yards; and the basque, 1½ yard.

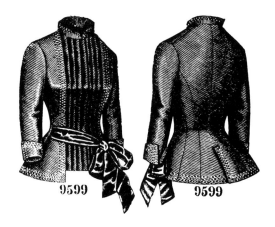

9599   **9599**

NO. 9599.—MISSES' BASQUE.—Another view of this basque, showing buttons and button-holes for closing, is given at figure No. 281 on page 68 of this issue. The pattern is in 8 sizes for misses from 8 to 15 years of age. To make the garment for a miss of 13 years, needs 3¼ yards of goods 22 inches wide, or 1½ yard 48 inches wide. Price of pattern. 10d. or 20 cents.

No. 9600. —MISSES' WALKING SKIRT.—At figure No. 281 on page 68,this walking skirt is again shown. The pattern is in 8 sizes for misses from 8 to 15 years of age. For a miss of 13 years, it needs 6⅝ yards of material 22 inches wide, or 3¼ yards 48 inches wide. Price of pattern, 1s. or 2 5 cents.

9600   **9600**

No. 9596.— MISSES' DRESS.— The dress here pictured is made of plain dark blue suiting, and braid and buttons comprise the trimming. Bands of contrasting goods or of plush, velvet or down may take the place of the skirt decoration pictured, if desired. The pattern is in 8 sizes for misses from 8 to 15 years of age. To make the dress for a miss of 13 years, will require 6⅝ yards of material 22 inches wide, or 3¼ yards of goods 48 inches wide. Price of pattern, 1s. 3d. or 30 cents.

9595   **9595**

9596   **9596**

No. 9595.—LADIES' COAT.—The stylishly shaped coat pictured in these engravings is made of heavy cloth and simply finished with fancy buttons as represented. The pattern is in 13 sizes for ladies from 28 to 46 inches, bust measure. To make the garment for a lady of medium size, will require 4¼ yards of goods 22 inches wide, or 1⅞ yard 48 inches wide, or 1¾ yard 54 inches wide. Price of pattern, 1s. 3d. or 30 cents.

9601   **9601**

No. 9601.—GIRLS' COSTUME.—At figure No.
271 on page 65, this stylish costume is again
prettily pictured. The pattern is in 8 sizes for
girls from 5 to 12 years of age. To make the
costume for a girl of 8 years, requires 5 yards
of material 22 inches wide, or 2⅜ yards 48
inches wide. Price of pattern, 1s. or 25 cents.

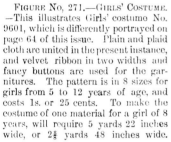

FIGURE No. 271.—GIRLS' COSTUME.
—This illustrates Girls' costume No.
9601, which is differently portrayed on
page 64 of this issue. Plain and plaid
cloth are united in the present instance,
and velvet ribbon in two widths and
fancy buttons are used for the garnitures. The pattern is in 8 sizes for
girls from 5 to 12 years of age, and
costs 1s. or 25 cents. To make the
costume of one material for a girl of 8
years, will require 5 yards 22 inches
wide, or 2⅜ yards 48 inches wide.

FIGURE No. 283.—LADIES' TOILETTE.—This consists of Ladies' basque No. 9608, two views of which are given on page
66; and skirt No. 9609, also shown on page 65. The basque
pattern is in 13 sizes for ladies from 28 to 46 inches, bust
measure, and costs 1s. or 25 cents. The skirt pattern is in 9
sizes for ladies from 20 to 36 inches, waist measure, and costs
1s. 3d. or 30 cents. For a lady of medium size, it requires 13¼
yards of material 22 inches wide: the basque needing 3½ yards;
and the skirt, 9¾ yards. Of goods 48 inches wide, 6¼ yards will
be needed: the basque requiring 1⅝ yard; and the skirt, 4⅝ yards.

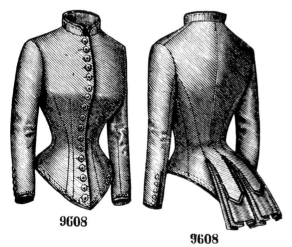

9608

9608

No. 9608.—LADIES' BASQUE.—This basque is also represented at figure No. 283 on page 68 of this publication. The
pattern is in 13 sizes for ladies from 28 to 46 inches, bust
measure. To make the garment for a lady of medium
size, will require 3½ yards of material 22 inches wide,
or 1⅝ yard 48 inches wide. Price of pattern, 1s. or 25 cents.

9609

No. 9609.—
LADIES' WALKING
SKIRT.—At figure
No. 283 on page
68, this skirt is
again shown. The
pattern is in 9
sizes for ladies
from 20 to 36 in-
ches, waist meas-
ure, and is here
employed for
brown cloth, with
a plaiting of the
same, pipings of
braid and ma-
chine-stitching for
its simple yet styl-
ish decorations. To
make the garment
for a lady of me-
dium size, will re-
quire 9¾ yards of
goods 22 inches
wide, or 4⅝ yards
of material 48 in-
ches wide. Price
of pattern, 1s. 3d.
or 30 cents.

9609

FIGURE No. 275.—CHILD'S COSTUME.—This illustrates Child's costume No. 9604, which is also shown elsewhere on this page. The pattern is in 5 sizes for children from 2 to 6 years of age. For a child of 6 years, it needs 4¼ yards of goods 22 inches wide, or 1⅞ yard 48 inches wide. Price of pattern, 7d. or 15 cents.

No. 9604.—CHILD'S COSTUME.—Another view of this costume may be observed at figure No. 275 shown elsewhere on this page. The pattern is in 5 sizes for children from 2 to 6 years of age, and is adapted to all varieties of seasonable dress goods. To make the costume for a child of 6 years, will require 4¼ yards of material 22 inches wide, or 1⅞ yard of goods 48 inches wide. Price of pattern, 7d. or 15 cents.

9604

9604

9602　　　**9602**

No. 9602.—LADIES' BASQUE.—This basque is again shown at figure No. 272 on page 66. Dark gray suiting was chosen for the construction in this instance. The straps contrast with the basque fabric, and either jet, steel, silver or gilt slides may be used. The pattern is in 13 sizes for ladies from 28 to 46 inches, bust measure. For a lady of medium size, it requires 3⅝ yards of material 22 inches wide, or 1¼ yard 48 inches wide. Price of pattern, 1s. or 25 cents.

9603

No. 9603.— LADIES' WALKING SKIRT. — Another illustration of this exceedingly stylish walking-skirt may be observed at figure No. 272 on page 66. Plain dress goods, with velvet for the straps and plaiting, are developed in the present instance. The pattern is in 9 sizes for ladies from 20 to 36 inches, waist measure. To make the garment for a lady of medium size, will require 11⅝ yards of material 22 inches wide, or 5⅝ yards of goods 48 inches wide. Price of pattern, 1s. 3d. or 30 cents.

9603

FIGURE No. 272.—LADIES' TOILETTE.—This consists of Ladies' basque No. 9602, which is represented in a different combination of material and trimming on page 65; and skirt No. 9603, illustrated in two views, showing another style of fabric and decoration on page 65. The basque pattern is in 13 sizes for ladies from 28 to 46 inches, bust measure, and costs 1s. or 25 cents. The skirt pattern is in 9 sizes for ladies from 20 to 36 inches, waist measure, and costs 1s. 3d. or 30 cents. For a lady of medium size, it will require 15 yards of material 22 inches wide: the basque requiring 3⅝ yards; and the skirt, 11⅜ yards.

No. 9616.—LADIES' SHIRRED WAIST.—Dress-bodies of the style illustrated in the above engravings are very becoming to slender figures. The pattern is in 13 sizes for ladies from 28 to 46 inches, bust measure, and may be employed for all varieties of goods that are not too heavy to permit of being shirred. To make the waist for a lady of medium size, requires 2⅞ yards of material 22 inches wide, or 1⅝ yard 36 inches wide, or 1¼ yard 48 inches wide, each with ⅝ yard of lining 36 inches wide for the fronts and back. Price of pattern, 7d. or 15 cents.

9616

9616

No. 9617.— LADIES' WRAP.—This garment is made of fancy cloth, with feather bands as trimmings. Fringe, fur, down or *passementerie* may replace the feather-band trimming. The pattern is in 10 sizes for ladies from 28 to 46 inches, bust measure. To make the garment for a lady of medium size, will require 4⅞ yards of material 22 inches wide, or 2 yards 48 inches wide, or 1⅞ yard 54 inches wide. Price of pattern, 1s. 3d. or 30 cents.

9617

9617

9606

9606

FIGURE No. 273.—LADIES' COSTUME.—This illustrates Ladies' costume No. 9606, which is represented in another material, with another arrangement of trimming, on page 65 of this issue. The pattern is in 13 sizes for ladies from 28 to 46 inches, bust measure. To make the costume of one material for a lady of medium size, will require 15¼ yards 22 inches wide, or 7¾ yards 48 inches wide. Price of pattern, 1s. 6d. or 35 cents.

No. 9606.—LADIES' COSTUME.—This handsome costume is further represented at figure No. 273 on page 66 of this issue. Velvet and woolen goods are combined in the present instance, and the decorations, which comprise velvet and crochetted buttons, are very tastefully disposed. It unites a nicely draped walking-skirt with a jaunty dress-body of pretty outlines. The pattern is in 13 sizes for ladies from 28 to 46 inches, bust measure. To make the garment for a lady of medium size, requires 10⅞ yards of material and 4⅝ yards of contrasting goods 22 inches wide, or 5⅜ yards of the one and 2¼ yards of the other 48 inches wide. Price of pattern, 1s. 6d. or 35 cents.

No. 9611.—CHILD'S NIGHT-DRAWERS.—This is a comfortably fashioned garment for little people's night-wear. The pattern is in 9 sizes for children from 2 to 10 years of age. For a child of 6 years, it requires 2⅞ yards of material 27 inches wide, or 2¼ yards of goods 36 inches wide. Price of pattern, 10d. or 20 cents.

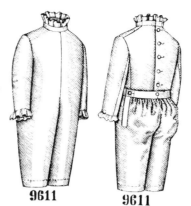

9611   **9611**

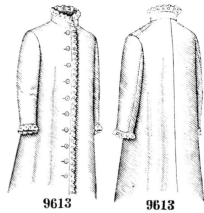

9613   **9613**

No. 9613.—GIRLS' CIRCULAR NIGHT-DRESS. —Fine muslin was employed for this night-dress, and embroidered edging forms the trimming. The pattern is in 7 sizes for girls from 3 to 9 years of age. To make the garment for a girl of 8 years, needs 2½ yards of material 36 inches wide. Price of pattern, 10d. or 20 cents.

9612

No. 9612.—MISSES' CIRCULAR NIGHT-DRESS.— The pretty and comfortably proportioned pattern shown in these engravings is in 8 sizes for misses from 8 to 15 years of age, and is here made of muslin, with lace edging and lace tucking for trimming. The edges may be decorated in any other manner desired, lace in the Valenciennes and *Torchon* varieties being most appropriate for such garments. To make the night-dress for a miss of 13 years, will require 3 yards of goods 36 inches wide. Price of pattern, 1s. or 25 cents.

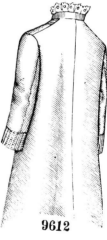

9612

FIGURE NO. 285.—MISSES' BOX-PLAITED CLOAK.— This illustrates Misses' box-plaited cloak No. 9610, other views of which may be observed by referring to page 67 of this issue. Dark green bourette cloth plaided with lines of crimson was selected for the construction of the garment in the present instance, with crimson velvet for the belt, pocket, collar and cuff-facings. Any other variety of cloaking may, however, be employed, and any different finish may be adopted. The pattern is in 8 sizes for misses from 8 to 15 years of age, and costs 1s. 3d. or 30 cents. To make the garment for a miss of 13 years, will require 6⅝ yards of material 22 inches wide, or 5¼ yards 27 inches wide, or 3¾ yards 48 inches wide.

No. 9610.— MISSES' BOX- PLAITED CLOAK.—This garment is again shown at figure No. 285 on page 68. The pattern is in 8 sizes for misses from 8 to 15 years of age. To make the cloak for a miss of 13 years, will require 6⅝ yards of material 22 inches wide, or 5¼ yards 27 inches wide. If goods 48 inches wide be chosen, then 3¾ yards will be sufficient. Price of pattern, 1s. 3d. or 30 cents.

9610   **9610**

GIRL DOLLS' SET NO. 97.—CONSISTING OF A HOUSE COSTUME AND FEDORA VEST.—At figure No. 263 on page 63 of this issue, these garments are again illustrated. The Set is in 7 sizes for dolls from 12 to 24 inches tall. For a girl doll 22 inches in height, the costume will need 1¼ yard of goods 22 inches wide, while the vest will require ⅜ yard of lace net 27 inches wide. Price of Set, 10d. or 20 cents.

9576

No. 9576.—GIRLS' TAM O'SHANTER CAP.—This pattern, which is again shown at figure No. 258 on page 63, is in 5 sizes for girls from 1 to 9 years of age. For a girl of 7 years, it will require ¾ yard of material 22 inches wide, or ½ yard 48 inches wide, together with ⅓ yard of silk 20 inches wide for lining. Price of pattern, 5d. or 10 cents.

FIGURE NO. 263.—GIRL DOLLS' HOUSE COSTUME.—This illustrates Girl Dolls' Set No. 97, which is again represented on page 61. The Set is in 7 sizes for dolls from 12 to 24 inches tall, and costs 10d. or 20 cents. For a girl doll 22 inches tall, it needs 1¼ yard of material 22 inches wide, with ⅜ yard of lace net 27 inches wide for the vest.

9614   **9614**

No. 9614.—GIRLS' COSTUME.—This costume is represented in other material at figure No. 277 on page 67. The pattern is in 8 sizes for girls from 5 to 12 years of age. For a girl of 8 years, it needs 4½ yards of material and 3 yards of contrasting goods, each 22 inches wide. Price of pattern, 1s. or 25 cents.

FIGURE NO. 277.—GIRLS' TOILETTE.—This consists of Girls' costume No. 9614, shown on page 64; and cap No. 9576, shown on page 64. The costume is in 8 sizes for girls from 5 to 12 years old, and costs 1s. or 25 cents. The cap is in 5 sizes for girls from 1 to 9 years old, and costs 5d. or 10 cents. For a girl of 8 years, they need 7¾ yards of goods 22 inches wide.

9618   **9618**

No. 9618.—GIRLS' MOTHER-HUBBARD APRON.—Another view of this pretty little garment is given at figure No. 269 on page 65 of this issue. The pattern is in 11 sizes for girls from 2 to 12 years of age. To make the apron for a girl of 8 years, will require 1⅝ yard of material 36 inches wide. Price of pattern, 7d. or 15 cents.

FIGURE NO. 248.—GIRL DOLLS' COSTUME, published January, 1882.—This is Girl Dolls' Set No. 75, also shown on page 58. Plaid suiting is here used for the dress, and plain goods for the cloak. The hood is a very jaunty accessory of the cloak and is lined with bright cardinal satin, a handsome tasselled ornament also being added at its point, The Set is in 7 sizes for dolls from 12 to 24 inches tall. For a girl doll 22 inches tall, the dress requires ½ yard of material 36 inches wide, while the cloak needs ⅝ yard 22 inches wide. Price of Set, 10d. or 20 cents.

FIGURE NO. 269.—GIRLS' MOTHER-HUBBARD APRON.—This illustrates Girls' apron No. 9618, which is shown with different trimming on page 64 of this issue. Nainsook is the material here used for it, and ruffles of the same form the garniture. All kinds of washable materials will make up handsomely by this pattern, and lace, embroidery or fancy edging may be chosen for decoration. The pattern is in 11 sizes for girls from 2 to 12 years of age. To make the garment for a girl of 8 years, will require 1⅝ yard of material 36 inches wide. Price of pattern 7d. or 15 cents.

No. 9619.— MISSES' JACKET.—This stylish jacket is again pictured at figure No. 276 on page 67. The pattern is in 8 sizes for misses from 8 to 15 years of age. To make the garment for a miss of 13 years, will require 3 yards of material 22 inches wide, or 2⅝ yards 27 inches wide, or 1½ yard 48 inches wide. Price of pattern, 10d. or 20 cents.

9619

9619

No. 9620.— LADIES' COAT.— These engravings portray an exceedingly handsome coat of check *frisé* goods, finished with machine-stitching. The pattern is in 13 sizes for ladies from 28 to 46 inches, bust measure. To make the garment for a lady of medium size, will require 4¾ yards of material 22 inches wide, or 2¼ yards 48 inches wide, or 2 yards 54 inches wide. Price of pattern, 1s. 3d. or 30 cents.

9620

9620

9621   **9621**

No. 9621.—CHILD'S JACKET.—This jacket is again shown at figure No. 284 elsewhere on this page. The pattern is in 5 sizes for children from 2 to 6 years of age. For a child of 6 years, it needs 2⅝ yards of goods 22 inches wide, or 2 yards 27 inches wide, or 1⅛ yard 48 inches wide. Price of pattern, 7d. or 15 cents.

FIGURE NO. 284.—CHILD'S STREET TOILETTE.—This consists of Child's jacket No. 9621, also shown elsewhere on this page; and costume No. 9106, again shown on page 43. The jacket pattern is in 5 sizes for children from 2 to 6 years of age, and costs 7d. or 15 cents. The costume pattern is in 7 sizes for girls from 3 to 9 years of age, and costs 10d. or 20 cents. To make the toilette of one material for a child of 6 years, will require 7½ yards 22 inches wide: the jacket needing 2⅝ yards; and the costume, 5⅛ yards.

9622

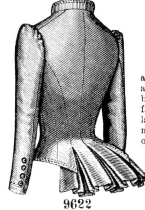

FIGURE NO. 276.—MISSES' STREET TOILETTE.— This consists of Misses' jacket No. 9619, which is again shown on page 66; and skirt No. 8641, also illustrated on page 46. The patterns are each in 8 sizes for misses from 8 to 15 years of age: the jacket costing 10d. or 20 cents; and the skirt, 1s. 3d. or 30 cents. For a miss of 13 years, they need 8½ yards of material 22 inches wide: the jacket requiring 3 yards; and the skirt, 5½ yards. If goods 48 inches wide be used, then 4⅝ yards will suffice: the jacket needing 1½ yard; and the skirt, 3⅛ yards.

No. 9622.—LADIES' BASQUE.—The above engravings show a basque made of twilled camel's-hair, with machine-stitching and bone buttons for trimming. Any seasonable suiting may be made up in a garment of this description, with braid or fancy galloon for trimming. The pattern is in 13 sizes for ladies from 28 to 46 inches, bust measure. For a lady of medium size, it requires 3½ yards of material 22 inches wide, or 1⅝ yard 48 inches wide. Price of pattern, 1s. or 25 cents.

9622

9624

No. 9 6 2 4 — LADIES' WRAP.—The accompanying engravings illustrate a very handsome street-garment made of seal-brown plush, with *écru* feather-band trimming as decoration about the neck, down each of the front and around the lower edges of the sleeves. The pattern is in 10 sizes for ladies from 28 to 46 inches, bust measure. To make the wrap for a lady of medium size, will require 4⅞ yards of material 22 inches wide, or 2 yards 48 inches wide, or 2 yards 54 inches wide. Price of pattern, 1s. or 25 cents.

9626

No. 9626.—STOCKING PATTERN.—Cashmere, cloth, stockinet, fine woolen goods or any other material desired may be made up in this way, with satisfactory results. The pattern is in 11 sizes for persons whose feet measure from 4 to 9 inches. To make a pair of stockings for feet 6½ inches in length, will require ¾ yard of material 27 inches wide. Price of pattern, 5d. or 10 cents.

9632 **9632**

No. 9632.—CHILD'S DRESS.—This dress is here made of fancy wash goods, with narrow colored embroidery for trimming. The pattern is in 5 sizes for children from 2 to 6 years of age. To make the garment for a child of 4 years, will need 3 yards of material 22 inches wide, or 2 yards 36 inches wide, or 1½ yard 48 inches wide. Price of pattern, 7d. or 15 cents.

9625 **9625**

No. 9625.—CHILD'S COSTUME. — The stylish-looking costume here illustrated is again shown at figure No. 282 elsewhere on this page. The pattern is in 5 sizes for children from 2 to 6 years of age. To make the costume for a child of 6 years, will require 5⅝ yards of material 22 inches wide, or 2½ yards 48 inches wide, each with ⅝ yard of Silesia 36 inches wide. Price of pattern, 7d. or 15 cents.

FIGURE NO. 282.—CHILD'S COSTUME.—This illustrates Child's costume No. 9625, again represented elsewhere on this page. Plaid and plain cloth and plain velvet are united in the present instance. The pattern is in 5 sizes for children from 2 to 6 years of age. To make the costume of one material for a child of 6 years, will require 5⅝ yards 22 inches wide, or 2½ yards 48 inches wide, each with ⅝ yard of Silesia 36 inches wide. Price of pattern, 7d. or 15 cents.

9623 **9623**

No. 9623.—GIRLS' CLOAK.—This garment is again shown at figure No. 279 on page 67. The pattern is in 8 sizes for girls from 5 to 12 years of age. For a girl of 8 years, it needs 3½ yards of goods 22 inches wide, or 1¾ yard 48 inches wide, with ½ yard of velvet 20 inches wide for the collar and straps. Price, 10d. or 20 cents.

FIGURE NO. 279.—GIRLS' CLOAK.—This illustrates Girls' cloak No. 9623, again pictured on page 64 of this issue. The pattern is in 8 sizes for girls from 5 to 12 years of age. For a girl of 8 years, it needs 3½ yards of material 22 inches wide, or 1¾ yard 48 inches wide, each with ½ yard of velvet 20 inches wide. Price of pattern, 10d. or 20 cents.

19

No. 9629.—LADIES' JACKET.—This jacket is made of fancy coating, with soutache braid along the edges and at the pocket openings. The pattern is in 13 sizes for ladies from 28 to 46 inches, bust measure, and is adapted to all kinds of cloths and coatings. Velvet or fancy bands may be used, with rich effect; or the finish may be severely plain. For a lady of medium size, it needs 3¾ yards of material 22 inches wide, or 1¾ yard 48 inches wide. Of 54-inch-wide goods, 1½ yard will be sufficient. Price of pattern, 1s. or 25 cents.

9629
9629

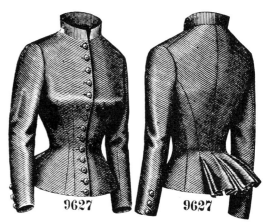

9627
9627

No. 9627.—LADIES' BASQUE.—Another view of this basque is given at figure No. 274 on page 66, where another material and different decorations are represented. The pattern is in 13 sizes for ladies from 28 to 46 inches, bust measure. To make the garment for a lady of medium size, will require 3¾ yards of material 22 inches wide. If goods 48 inches wide be chosen for it, then 1⅝ yard will be sufficient. Price of pattern, 1s. or 25 cents.

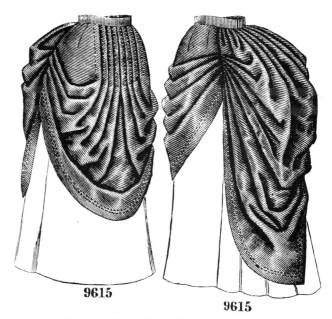

9615
9615

FIGURE NO. 274.—LADIES' TOILETTE.—This consists of Ladies' basque No. 9627, pictured on page 67; over-skirt No. 9615, shown on page 67; and skirt No. 8682, seen on page 28. The patterns to the skirt and over-skirt are each in 9 sizes for ladies from 20 to 36 inches, waist measure: the skirt costing 1s. 3d. or 30 cents; and the over-skirt, 1s. or 25 cents. The basque pattern is in 13 sizes for ladies from 28 to 46 inches, bust measure, and costs 1s. or 25 cents. For a lady of medium size, they need 13½ yards of goods 22 inches wide: the basque requiring 3⅝ yards; the over-skirt, 5⅝ yards; and the skirt, 4½ yards.

No. 9615.—LADIES' OVER-SKIRT.—Another illustration of this stylish over-skirt may be seen by referring to figure No. 274 on page 66 of this issue. Brown suiting was the material used for it in the present instance, with machine-stitching for trimming. The pattern is in 9 sizes for ladies from 20 to 36 inches, waist measure. To make the garment for a lady of medium size, will require 5⅝ yards of material 22 inches wide, or 2⅝ yards of goods 48 inches wide. Price of pattern, 1s. or 25 cents.

FIGURE NO. 278.—BOYS' DOUBLE-BREASTED OVERCOAT.—This illustrates Boys' overcoat No. 9628, which is shown in two views on page 68 of the present issue. Cheviot overcoating is the material here portrayed, and the finish is machine-stitching. The pattern is in 9 sizes for boys from 2 to 10 years of age, and is adapted to all varieties of light and heavy overcoatings. For a boy of 6 years, it requires 2¼ yards of material 27 inches wide. Price of pattern, 10d. or 20 cents.

9628   9628

NO. 9628.—BOYS' DOUBLE-BREASTED OVERCOAT, BUTTONED TO THE THROAT.—This overcoat is again shown at figure No. 278 on page 67. The pattern is in 9 sizes for boys from 2 to 10 years of age. For a boy of 6 years, it needs 2½ yards of material 27 inches wide. Price of pattern, 10d. or 20 cents.

9633   9633

NO. 9633.—GIRLS' DRESS.—The above engravings portray a really charming little dress for a girl. The pattern is in 7 sizes for girls from 3 to 9 years of age. To make the garment for a girl of 8 years, requires 2⅞ yards of material 22 inches wide, or 1⅜ yard of goods 48 inches wide. Price of pattern, 10d. or 20 cents.

9630   9630

NO. 9630.—CHILD'S SHIRT.—Fine white muslin was employed in the construction of the garment here illustrated. The pattern is in 7 sizes for children from 6 months to 6 years of age. For a child of 6 years, it requires 1¼ yard of goods 36 inches wide. Price of pattern, 5d. or 10 cents.

9634

NO. 9634.—LADIES' CHEMISE.—Linen, cambric, muslin or any preferred white goods may be chosen for the construction of a garment of this description. Fine bleached muslin was selected for its development in the present instance, and narrow embroidered edging provides the trimming. The pattern is in 10 sizes for ladies from 28 to 46 inches, bust measure. To make the chemise for a lady of medium size, will require 2⅞ yards of material 36 inches wide. Price of pattern, 10d. or 20 cents.

9634

9635

NO. 9635.—CHILD'S CHEMISE.—This chemise is here illustrated as made of fine cambric, with narrow embroidered edging as the decoration. Muslin, lawn, nainsook, flannel, merino or any material suitable for underclothing may be made up in this way, and any pretty trimming may be added. The pattern is in 6 sizes for children from 1 to 6 years of age. To make the garment for a child of 4 years, needs 1⅛ yard of goods 36 inches wide. Price of pattern, 5d. or 10 cts.

9638

NO. 9638.—LADIES' CIRCULAR NIGHT-DRESS.—Fine cambric was used for this garment, and lace edging and lace tucking forms the trimming. The pattern is in 10 sizes for ladies from 28 to 46 inches, bust measure. Embroidery or other wash trimming may take the place of the lace, if desired. To make the garment for a lady of medium size, requires 3⅞ yards of material 36 inches wide. Price of pattern, 1s. 3d. or 30 cents.

9638

No. 9639.—INFANTS' MOTHER-HUBBARD DRESS.—This
dainty little garment is made of nainsook and prettily
trimmed with lace edging in two widths, lace insertion
and clusters of tucks. Lawn of any preferred quality
may be selected for the construction of garments of
this description. The pattern is in one size, and, to
make a garment like it, calls for 2½ yards of material
36 inches wide. Price of pattern, 10d. or 20 cents.

9639   9639

9637   9637

No. 9637.—INFANTS' SLIP.—Fine muslin was the material
employed for the construction of the dainty garment here
represented, and clusters of tucks and embroidered edging
form the trimming. Nainsook, cambric, lawn, dimity or any
preferred fabric suitable for infants' use may be made up in
this way, and any desired garniture may be added. The pattern is in one size, and, for a garment like it, needs 2½ yards
of material 36 inches wide. Price of pattern, 7d. or 15 cents.

9631   9631

FIGURE NO. 268.—LADIES' STREET TOILETTE.—This
consists of Ladies' costume No. 9631, seen in other material on this page; and cape No. 9532, again shown on page
9. The costume pattern is in 13 sizes for ladies from
28 to 46 inches, bust measure, and costs 1s. 6d. or 35 cents.
The cape pattern is in 10 sizes for ladies from 28 to 46
inches, bust measure, and costs 7d. or 15 cents. For a
lady of medium size, the cape needs 1¼ yard of material
27 inches wide, or ⅝ yard either 48 or 54 inches wide,
each with 1½ yard of quilted satin 20 inches wide for lining.
For a lady of the same size, the costume needs 10¾ yards
of goods 22 inches wide, or 5⅛ yards 48 inches wide.

No. 9631.—LADIES' COSTUME.—Another illustration of this stylish costume, showing a combination of mode-colored canvas-cloth and seal-brown velvet, may be observed at figure No. 268 elsewhere on this page. Basket-pattern cloth is the material
here represented, with a knife-plaiting of the same and crochetted buttons for
trimming. The pattern is in 13 sizes for ladies from 28 to 46 inches, bust measure,
and may be selected for any dress goods in vogue, two varieties of material being
extremely effective when developed in this way. To make the costume for
a lady of medium size, will require 10¾ yards of material 22 inches wide,
or 5⅛ yards of goods 48 inches wide. Price of pattern, 1s. 6d. or 35 cents.

No. 9642.—
Ladies' Coat.
—This pattern
is in 13 sizes for
ladies from 28
to 46 inches,
bust measure,
and may be
used for cloths
and coatings of
all kinds. For
a lady of me-
dium size, it re-
quires 4 yards
of material 22
inches wide, or
1⅞ yard 48 in-
ches wide, or
1⅝ yard 54
inches wide.
Price of pat-
tern, 1s. 3d.
or 30 cents.

9642   **9642**

No. 9643.—Ladies'
Coat.—Cloth is the
material employed
for the coat shown
in these engravings,
and braid and buttons
form the neat and
tasteful trimmings.
The pattern is in 13
sizes for ladies from
28 to 46 inches, bust
measure. To make
the garment for a
lady of medium size,
will require 3⅝ yards
of material 22 inches
wide, or 1⅝ yard 48
inches wide, or 1⅓
yard 54 inches wide.
Price of pattern,
1s. 3d. or 30 cents.

9643   **9643**

No. 9640.—
Ladies' Coat.—
At figure No. 270
on page 65, an-
other illustration
of this garment
may be observed.
Dark brown cloth
is the material
illustrated in the
present instance,
with buttons and
a handsome braid-
ornament for trim-
ming. Any variety
of coating may,
however, be
chosen for it, and
any pleasing finish
adopted. Velvet
upon the collar
and about the
wrists would com-
plete such a gar-
ment tastefully.
The pattern is in
13 sizes for ladies
from 28 to 46 in-
ches, bust meas-
ure. To make the
coat for a lady of
medium size, will
require 7¼ yards
of material 22 in-
ches wide, or 3⅜
yards 48 inches
wide, or 3¼ yards
54 inches wide.
Price of pattern,
1s. 3d. or 30 cents.

9640   **9640**

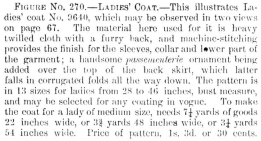

Figure No. 270.—Ladies' Coat.—This illustrates Ladies' coat No. 9640, which may be observed in two views
on page 67. The material here used for it is heavy
twilled cloth with a furry back, and machine-stitching
provides the finish for the sleeves, collar and lower part of
the garment; a handsome *passementerie* ornament being
added over the top of the back skirt, which latter
falls in corrugated folds all the way down. The pattern is
in 13 sizes for ladies from 28 to 46 inches, bust measure,
and may be selected for any coating in vogue. To make
the coat for a lady of medium size, needs 7¼ yards of goods
22 inches wide, or 3⅜ yards 48 inches wide, or 3¼ yards
54 inches wide. Price of pattern, 1s. 3d. or 30 cents.

FIGURE No. 280.—MISSES' PRINCESS DRESS.—This illustrates Misses' dress No. 9641, two views of which are given elsewhere on this page. Plain and embroidered cashmere are the materials illustrated in the present instance, the plain variety being employed for the entire dress-portion and the embroidered goods for the drapery. The pattern is in 8 sizes for misses from 8 to 15 years of age. To make the dress of one material for a miss of 13 years, will require $8\frac{5}{8}$ yards 22 inches wide, or $4\frac{1}{8}$ yards 48 inches wide. Price of pattern, 1s. 3d. or 30 cents.

No. 9656.—MISSES' KNICKERBOCKER DRAWERS.—This pattern is in 8 sizes for misses from 8 to 15 years old. For a miss of 13 years, it needs $1\frac{3}{4}$ yard 36 inches wide. Price, 7d. or 15 cents.

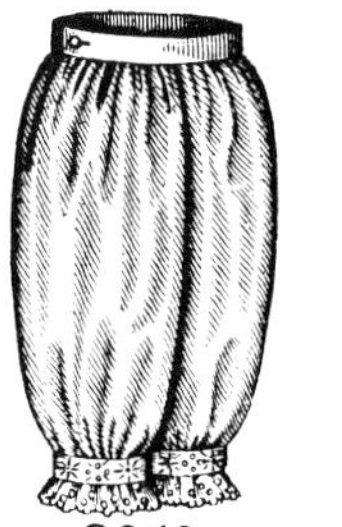

9656

9650

No. 9650.—LADIES' WRAP.—This pattern is in 10 sizes for ladies from 28 to 46 inches, bust measure. For a lady of medium size, it needs $2\frac{1}{8}$ yards of goods 22 inches wide, or $1\frac{1}{3}$ yard 48 inches wide, or $1\frac{1}{8}$ yard 54 inches wide. Price of pattern, 1s. or 25 cents.

9650

9641

No. 9641.—MISSES' PRINCESS DRESS, WITH DRAPERY.—This garment is differently pictured at figure No. 280 elsewhere on this page. The pattern is in 8 sizes for misses from 8 to 15 years of age. Any preferred decoration may take the place of that here illustrated. For a miss of 13 years, it will require $8\frac{5}{8}$ yards of material 22 inches wide, or $4\frac{1}{8}$ yards of goods 48 inches wide. Price of pattern, 1s. 3d. or 30 cents.

9641

FIGURE No. 292.—LADIES' COSTUME.—This illustrates Ladies' costume No. 9652, which is portrayed in two views, showing a combination of plain and brocaded goods, on page 69 of this publication. Three materials—plain and brocaded silk and plain velvet—are combined in the present instance. The skirt is made of the plain silk and trimmed with three narrow knife-plaitings of the same, and the handsome *tablier*-drapery is of the brocaded goods. The pattern is in 13 sizes for ladies from 28 to 46 inches, bust measure. To make the costume of one material for a lady of medium size, will require $15\frac{1}{3}$ yards 22 inches wide, or $7\frac{5}{8}$ yards 48 inches wide. Price of pattern, 1s. 6d. or 35 cents.

No. 9652.—LADIES' COSTUME.—This costume is again shown at figure No. 292 on page 70 of this issue. Plain silk and brocaded velvet are united in the present instance. The pattern is in 13 sizes for ladies from 28 to 46 inches, bust measure. For a lady of medium size, it needs 6⅞ yards of plain goods and 8¼ yards of brocaded material 22 inches wide, or 3⅝ yards of the one and 4 yards of the other 48 inches wide. Price of pattern, 1s. 6d. or 35 cents.

9652

9652

FIGURE NO. 288.—LADIES' COSTUME.—This illustrates Ladies' costume No. 9644, which is shown with a different style of decoration on page 72. The costume is very stylish, and is here developed in twilled English serge of a moss-green shade, with a narrow foot-plaiting, soutache braid and buttons for its garnitures. The pattern is in 13 sizes for ladies from 28 to 46 inches, bust measure. To make the costume for a lady of medium size, will require 10¾ yards of material 22 inches wide, or 5⅝ yards 48 inches wide. Price of pattern, 1s. 6d. or 35 cents.

9644

9644

No. 9644.—LADIES' COSTUME.—At figure No. 288 on page 69, another view of this costume is given. The pattern is in 13 sizes for ladies from 28 to 46 inches, bust measure, and is here used for plain gray suit goods, with a box-plaiting of the same about the foot of the skirt. For a lady of medium size, it needs 10¾ yards of goods 22 inches wide, or 5⅝ yards 48 inches wide. Price of pattern, 1s. 6d. or 35 cents.

FIGURE NO. 289.—GIRLS' COSTUME. —This illustrates Girls' costume No. 9663, which is portrayed in a different combination of material and decoration on page 70. The pattern is in 8 sizes for girls from 5 to 12 years of age. Of one material for a girl of 8 years, it needs 5½ yards 22 inches wide, or 2½ yards 48 inches wide. As here pictured, it will require 2¾ yards of goods 22 inches wide for the skirt, with 2½ yards of velvet 20 inches wide for the jacket, and ⅜ yard of silk 20 inches wide for the vest and standing collar. Price of pattern, 1s. or 25 cents.

9654 **9654**

NO. 9654.—LADIES' COSTUME.—This stylish costume is made of cloth, with the material, velvet bands and facings and tinsel braid for decorations. Any other arrangement of skirt trimming admired may, however, take the place of that here pictured. The pattern is in 13 sizes for ladies from 28 to 46 inches, bust measure. To make the costume, without the folds and box-plaiting represented, for a lady of medium size, requires 10⅝ yards of goods 22 inches wide, or 5⅜ yards 48 inches wide. Price of pattern, 1s. 6d. or 35 cents.

No. 9663.— GIRLS' COSTUME. —This pattern, again shown at figure No. 289 on page 69, is in 8 sizes for girls from 5 to 12 years of age. For a girl of 8 years, it requires 5½ yards of material 22 inches wide. As pictured, it needs 2¾ yards of goods 22 inches wide, with 2½ yards of velvet and ⅜ yard of Ottoman silk. Price, 1s. or 25 cents.

9645

9663

9645

FIGURE NO. 295.—MISSES' COSTUME.—This illustrates Misses' costume No. 9645, which is shown in another material on page 69 of this issue. The pattern is in 8 sizes for misses from 8 to 15 years of age, and costs 1s. 3d. or 30 cents. For a miss of 13 years, it will need 11⅝ yards of material 22 inches wide.

NO. 9645.—MISSES' COSTUME.—Another view of this garment is given at figure No. 295 on page 71, where it is made of plain cloth and velvet. The pattern is in 8 sizes for misses from 8 to 15 years of age. For a miss of 13 years, it needs 10½ yards of one fabric and 1½ yard of contrasting goods 22 inches wide, or 4⅝ yards of the one and ⅜ yard of the other 48 inches wide. Price of pattern, 1s. 3d. or 30 cents.

9663

No. 9648.—Ladies' Basque.—Another view of this garment is given at figure No. 304 on this page. The pattern is in 13 sizes for ladies from 28 to 46 inches, bust measure, and may be chosen for any fashionable dress goods. To make the basque for a lady of medium size, will require 3⅝ yards of goods 22 inches wide, or 1¾ yard 48 inches wide. Price of pattern, 1s. or 25 cents.

9648

9648

9649   **9649**

No. 9649.—Girls' Jacket.—This jacket is again shown at figure No. 290 on page 69. The pattern is in 7 sizes for girls from 3 to 9 years of age. For a girl of 8 years, it needs 2⅝ yards of one material and 1 yard of contrasting goods 22 inches wide. Price of pattern, 7d. or 15 cents.

Figure No. 290.—Girls' Street Toilette.—This consists of Girls' jacket No. 9649, again shown on page 68; and costume No. 9106, represented on page 43. The jacket pattern is in 7 sizes for girls from 3 to 9 years of age, and costs 7d. or 15 cents. The costume pattern is in 7 sizes for girls from 3 to 9 years of age, and costs 10d. or 20 cents. Of one material for a girl of 8 years, they will require 9⅞ yards 22 inches wide: the jacket needing 3⅝ yards; and the costume, 6¼ yards.

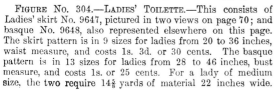

Figure No. 304.—Ladies' Toilette.—This consists of Ladies' skirt No. 9647, pictured in two views on page 70; and basque No. 9648, also represented elsewhere on this page. The skirt pattern is in 9 sizes for ladies from 20 to 36 inches, waist measure, and costs 1s. 3d. or 30 cents. The basque pattern is in 13 sizes for ladies from 28 to 46 inches, bust measure, and costs 1s. or 25 cents. For a lady of medium size, the two require 14⅝ yards of material 22 inches wide.

No. 9647.—Ladies' Walking Skirt.—This skirt is represented in an entirely different combination of materials and with other decorations at figure No. 304 on page 72. Plain and brocaded Ottoman are here united, and a plaiting of the plain Ottoman, ruffles of lace and *passementerie* ornaments comprise the trimming. The pattern is in 9 sizes for ladies from 20 to 36 inches, waist measure, and is adapted to any style of dress goods in vogue. For a lady of medium size, it needs 8⅝ yards of plain material and 2⅜ yards of brocaded goods 22 inches wide, or 4½ yards of plain and 1 yard of brocaded 48 inches wide. Price of pattern, 1s. 3d. or 30 cents.

9647   **9647**

FIGURE NO. 313.—GIRLS'
COAT.—This is Girls' coat No.
9651, seen on page 70. The pattern is in 7 sizes for girls from
3 to 9 years old, and costs 10d. or
20 cents. For a girl of 8 years, it
needs 3⅞ yards 22 inches wide.

No. 9651.—
GIRLS' COAT.—At
figure No. 313 on
page 74 of this
issue, this coat is
again illustrated.
The pattern is in
7 sizes for girls
from 3 to 9 years
of age. To make
the coat for a girl
of 8 years, will
require 3⅞ yards
of material 22
inches wide, or
1¾ yard 48 in-
ches wide. Price
of pattern, 10d.
or 20 cents.

9651

9651

9655   **9655**

NO. 9655.—MISSES' POLONAISE.—At figure No. 315 on
page 74, this polonaise may again be seen. The pattern
is in 8 sizes for misses from 8 to 15 years of age, and may
be employed for any seasonable dress goods. For a miss
of 13 years, it needs 6⅝ yards of material 22 inches wide,
or 3⅜ yards 48 inches wide. Price of pattern, 1s. or 25 cents.

FIGURE NO. 315.—MISSES' POLONAISE COSTUME.—This
consists of Misses' polonaise No. 9655, also shown on
page 73; and skirt No. 8082, again shown on page 46.
Both patterns are in 8 sizes for misses from 8 to 15 years
of age, and each costs 1s. or 25 cents. For a miss of 13
years, they need 10⅝ yards of material 22 inches wide.

No. 9646.—
LADIES' WRAP.
—This pattern
is in 10 sizes for
ladies from 28
to 46 inches.
bust measure.
To make the
wrap for a lady
of medium
size, will re-
quire 4 yards
of plain mate-
rial 22 inches
wide, with ⅜
yard of bead-
ed lace net
27 inches wide
and ¼ yard
of silk 20 in-
ches wide. Of
one material,
it will require
4¾ yards 22
inches wide,
or 1⅞ yard 48
inches wide.
Price of pat-
tern, 1s. 3d.
or 30 cents.

9646   **9646**

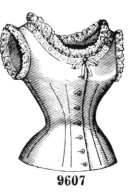

9607

9607

NO. 9607.—LADIES' CORSET-COVER.—This pattern is in 13
sizes for ladies from 28 to 46 inches, bust measure, and may
be employed for any material usually selected for underclothing. The garment may be in low-necked, sleeveless style,
or it may be made with a high neck and long sleeves, as
preferred. To make the corset-cover with the sleeves and a
high neck for a lady of medium size, requires 1¾ yard
of material 36 inches wide. Price of pattern, 10d. or 20 cents.

28

No. 9658.—
Child's Dress.—
This pattern,
again shown at
figure No. 298 on
page 71, is in 5
sizes for children
from 2 to 6 years
of age. For a
child of 6 years, it
needs 3 yards of
goods 22 inches
wide, or 1⅞ yard
36 inches wide,
or 1⅜ yard 48 in-
ches wide. Price,
7d. or 15 cents.

9658

9658

FIGURE No. 298.—Child's Plain
Dress.—This pictures Child's dress
No. 9658, shown on page 70. The
pattern is in 5 sizes for children from
2 to 6 years of age. For a child of 6
years, it needs 3 yards of goods 22
inches wide, or 1⅜ yard 48 inches
wide. Price of pattern, 7d. or 15 cents.

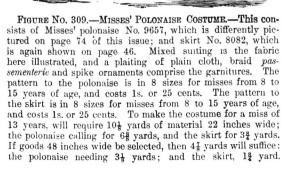

FIGURE No. 309.—Misses' Polonaise Costume.—This consists of Misses' polonaise No. 9657, which is differently pictured on page 74 of this issue; and skirt No. 8082, which
is again shown on page 46. Mixed suiting is the fabric
here illustrated, and a plaiting of plain cloth, braid *passementerie* and spike ornaments comprise the garnitures. The
pattern to the polonaise is in 8 sizes for misses from 8 to
15 years of age, and costs 1s. or 25 cents. The pattern to
the skirt is in 8 sizes for misses from 8 to 15 years of age,
and costs 1s. or 25 cents. To make the costume for a miss of
13 years, will require 10¼ yards of material 22 inches wide;
the polonaise calling for 6⅜ yards, and the skirt for 3¾ yards.
If goods 48 inches wide be selected, then 4⅞ yards will suffice:
the polonaise needing 3⅜ yards; and the skirt, 1¼ yard.

9657

9657

No. 9657.—Misses' Polonaise.—Another illustration of
this over-dress may be seen at figure No. 309 on page 73.
The back of the garment shows the straight folds character-
izing the waterfall style of drapery. The pattern is in 8
sizes for misses from 8 to 15 years of age. For a miss of 13
years, it needs 6⅜ yards of goods 22 inches wide, or 3¼
yards 48 inches wide. Price of pattern, 1s. or 25 cents.

Fig. No. 312.—Child's Costume.—This is Child's costume
No. 9674, seen on page 68. The
pattern is in 5 sizes from 2 to 6
years. For a child of 6 years.
it needs 3¼ yards 22 inches
wide. Price, 7d. or 15 cents.

9674

No. 9674.—Child's Street Costume,
with Removable Cape.—This pattern,
again shown at figure No. 312 on page 74,
is in 5 sizes for children from 2 to 6 years of
age. For a child of 6 years, it needs 3¼ yards
of goods 22 inches wide, or 2½ yards 27 inches wide. Price of pattern, 7d. or 15 cents.

9674

9660

No. 9660.—CHILD'S COSTUME.—This costume is again shown at figure No. 302 on page 72. The pattern is in 5 sizes for children from 2 to 6 years old. For a child of 6 years, it needs 4 yards of one fabric and ⅞ yard of contrasting goods 22 inches wide. Price, 10d. or 20 cents.

9660

FIGURE No. 302. — CHILD'S COSTUME.—This illustrates Child's costume No. 9660, also seen on page 68. The pattern is in 5 sizes for children from 2 to 6 years old, and costs 10d. or 20 cts. For a child of 6 years, it needs 4⅞ yards of goods 22 inches wide.

FIGURE NO. 264.—LADY DOLLS' STREET COSTUME.—This illustrates Lady Dolls' Set No. 95, which is differently represented on page 64 of this issue. The Set is in 7 sizes for dolls from 12 to 24 inches in height. To make the costume for a lady doll 22 inches tall, will require 1⅝ yard of material 22 inches wide. Price of Set, 7d. or 15 cents.

FIGURE NO. 301.—LADIES' COSTUME.—This illustrates Ladies' costume No. 9659, which is pictured in two views, showing a different material and another arrangement of braid trimming, on page 69. The pattern is in 13 sizes for ladies from 28 to 46 inches, bust measure, and costs 1s. 6d. or 35 cents. For a lady of medium size, it needs 13 yards of material 22 inches wide, or 6¼ yards 48 inches wide.

9659   **9659**

No. 9659.—LADIES' COSTUME.—Another view of this costume is given at figure No. 301 on page 72 of this issue. Plain dress goods were used in this instance, with a plaiting of the same, narrow braid and crochetted buttons for decorations. The pattern is in 13 sizes for ladies from 28 to 46 inches, bust measure. For a lady of medium size, it needs 13 yards of goods 22 inches wide, or 6½ yards 48 inches wide. Price of pattern, 1s. 6d. or 35 cents.

9661   **9661**

No. 9661.—Child's Wrap.—At figure No. 303 on page 72, another view of this little wrap may be seen. The pattern is in 5 sizes for children from 2 to 6 years of age. For a child of 6 years, it needs 3⅝ yards of material 22 inches wide, or 1⅝ yard 48 inches wide. Price of pattern, 7d. or 15 cents.

Figure No. 303. — Child's Wrap.—This illustrates Child's wrap No. 9661, also seen on page 68. The pattern is in 5 sizes for children from 2 to 6 years old, and costs 7d. or 15 cents. For a child of 6 years, it needs 3⅝ yards of goods 22 inches wide

No. 9677.—Child's Night-Drawers, with Stockings.—Bleached muslin was employed for this garment. The pattern is in 10 sizes for children from 1 to 10 years of age. To make the garment for a child of 8 years, will require 3½ yards of material 27 inches wide, or 2⅞ yards 36 inches wide. Price of pattern, 10d. or 20 cents.

9677   **9677**

9670   **9670**

No. 9670.—Misses' Costume.—This is a most attractive style of costume for a miss. The pattern is in 8 sizes for misses from 8 to 15 years of age. For a miss of 13 years, it needs 3¼ yards of plain material and 5½ yards of brocaded goods 22 inches wide, or 1¾ yard of the one and 2⅝ yards of the other 48 inches wide. Price of pattern, 1s. 3d. or 30 cents.

9676   **9676**

No. 9676.—Infants' Bib.—This pretty little pattern is in one size; and, to make half a dozen bibs like it, will require 1¼ yard of material 36 inches wide, with 1¼ yard of lining goods in the same width. Price of pattern, 5d. or 10 cents.

No. 9653.— Ladies' Polonaise. — Spring suiting and contrasting velvet are the materials united in the construction of the stylish garment shown in these engravings, the latter fabric, buttons and ornamental button-holes providing the garnitures. The pattern is in 13 sizes for ladies from 28 to 46 inches, bust measure, and may be used for a combination of materials, or for a single variety, as desired. To make the polonaise for a lady of medium size, will require 7½ yards of one material and ⅞ yard of another 22 inches wide. or 3⅝ yards of the one and ⅞ yard of the other 48 inches wide. Price of pattern 1s. 3d. or 30 cents.

9653   **9653**

9664   **9664**

No. 9664.—Misses' Coat.—The pattern to the coat here depicted is in 8 sizes for misses from 8 to 15 years of age, and is here used for cloth, with narrow braid for decoration. For a miss of 13 years, it needs 5⅛ yards of goods 22 inches wide, or 2⅝ yards 48 inches wide. Price of pattern, 1s. or 25 cents.

9684   **9684**

No. 9684.—Miss-es' Basque.—The pattern to this basque is in 8 sizes for misses from 8 to 15 years of age. To make the garment for a miss of 13 years, requires 2¼ yards of goods 22 inches wide, or 1½ yard 36 inches wide, or 1⅛ yard 48 inches wide. Price of pattern, 10d. or 20 cents.

9688   **9688**

No. 9688.—Boys' Coat.—This pattern is in 8 sizes for boys from 5 to 12 years of age, and may be used for all varieties of coatings. For a boy of 9 years, it will require 2 yards of material 27 inches wide. Price of pattern, 10d. or 20 cents.

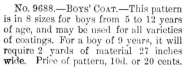

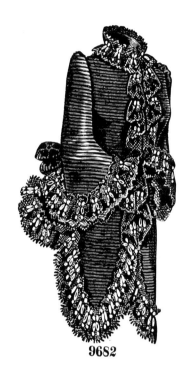

No. 9682.—Ladies' Wrap.—Plain and brocaded Ottoman are united in the handsome wrap pictured. The pattern is in 10 sizes for ladies from 28 to 46 inches, bust measure. For a lady of medium size, it requires 3½ yards of plain goods and 1 yard of brocaded material 22 inches wide, or 1¼ yard of the one and ¾ yard of the other 48 inches wide. Price of pattern, 1s. 3d. or 30 cents.

9682   **9682**

9662   **9662**

9687

No. 9687.—Boys' Four-Button Cut-away Coat.—The pattern to this jaunty little coat is in 9 sizes for boys from 7 to 15 years of age. To make the garment for a boy of 11 years, needs 2⅝ yards of goods 27 inches wide. Price of pattern, 1s. or 25 cents.

9687

Figure No. 305.—Misses' Costume.—This illustrates Misses' costume No. 9662, also shown on page 74. The pattern is in 8 sizes for misses from 8 to 15 years old, and costs 1s. 3d. or 30 cents. For a miss of 13 years, it needs 9⅝ yards of goods 22 inches wide, or 4⅛ yards 48 inches wide.

No. 9662.—Misses' Costume.—This costume is also represented at figure No. 305 on page 72. The pattern is in 8 sizes for misses from 8 to 15 years of age, and may be chosen for any fashionable suiting. To make the costume for a miss of 13 years, will require 9⅝ yards of goods 22 inches wide, or 4⅛ yards 48 inches wide. Price of pattern, 1s. 3d. or 30 cents.

No. 9671.—
GIRLS' COSTUME.
—This little cos-
tume is here made
of plain suiting.
The pattern is in 7
sizes for girls from
3 to 9 years of age,
and may be used
for all kinds of
dress goods. For
a girl of 8 years, it
needs 4⅝ yards of
goods 22 inches
wide, or 2⅛ yards
48 inches wide.
Price of pattern,
10d. or 20 cents.

9671   **9671**

No. 9686.—
LADIES' OVER-
SKIRT.—Plain
dress goods of
a medium tex-
ture were em-
ployed for this
over-skirt, and
machine-
stitching gives
a neat and
tasteful fin-
ish. The pat-
tern is in 9 sizes
for ladies from
20 to 36 inches,
waistmeasure.
For a lady of
medium size,
it will require
6 yards of
goods 22 inch-
es wide, or 4
yards 36 inch-
es wide, or 3¼
yards 48 inch-
es wide. Price
of pattern, 1s.
or 25 cents.

9686   **9686**

No. 9698.—BOYS'
SINGLE – BREASTED
SACK COAT.—Fancy
cloth was employed
for the coat here pic-
tured. The pattern
is in 8 sizes for boys
from 5 to 12 years
of age. To make the
garment for a boy
of 9 years, will re-
quire 2 yards of ma-
terial 27 inches wide.
Price of pattern,
10d. or 20 cents.

9698   **9698**

9665   **9665**

FIGURE NO. 314.—LADIES' ULSTER.—This illustrates
Ladies' Ulster No. 9665, which is again represented on
page 72 of this issue. A stylish variety of Spring Cheviot was selected for the garment in this instance, with
machine-stitching and buttons for trimming. The pattern is in 10 sizes for ladies from 28 to 46 inches, bust
measure, and costs 1s. 3d. or 30 cents. For a lady of medium size, it requires 8¼ yards of goods 22 inches wide, or
3½ yards 48 inches wide, or 3¼ yards 54 inches wide.

No. 9665.—LADIES' ULSTER.—Another view of this Ulster may
be seen at figure No. 314 on page 74. The pattern is in 10 sizes for
ladies from 28 to 46 inches, bust measure. For a lady of medium size,
it needs 8¼ yards of material 22 inches wide, or 3½ yards 48 inches
wide, or 3¼ yards 54 inches wide. Price of pattern, 1s. 3d. or 30 cents.

9695   9695

No. 9695.—Boys' Yachting Trousers. —This pattern is in 9 sizes for boys from 7 to 15 years of age. For a boy of 11 years, it needs 2½ yards of goods 27 inches wide, with ¼ yard of stay linen 33 inches wide. Price of pattern, 7d. or 15 cents.

9691

No. 9691.—Boys' Vest, with Shawl Collar.—This vest is here made of fancy striped suiting and finished with machine-stitching. The pattern is in 9 sizes for boys from 7 to 15 years of age. For a boy of 11 years, it needs ⅝ yard of material 27 inches wide, with ½ yard of Silesia 36 inches wide. Price, 5d. or 10 cts.

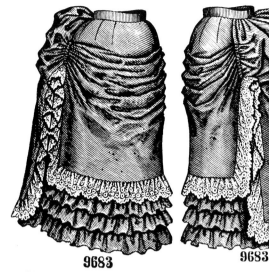

9683   9683

No. 9683.—Misses' Walking Skirt.—Plain blue gingham is here made up, and lace is used for decorating the drapery edges, while ruffles of the material trim the skirt. The pattern is in 8 sizes for misses from 8 to 15 years of age. For a miss of 13 years, it will require 5⅞ yards of goods 22 inches wide, or 3⅜ yards 48 inches wide. Price of pattern, 1s. or 25 cents.

Figure No. 296.—Misses' Coat.—This pictures Misses' coat No. 9666, shown again elsewhere on this page. The pattern is in 8 sizes for misses from 8 to 15 years of age. For a miss of 13 years, it needs 5½ yards of goods 22 inches wide. Price of pattern, 1s. or 25 cents.

9675

No. 9675.—Infants' Slip.—Cambric was employed for the construction of the little garment represented in the accompanying engravings, and narrow embroidered edging added to the neck and wrists forms the simple but tasteful garniture. The pattern is in one size, and, in making a garment like it, 1⅞ yard of material 36 inches wide will be sufficient. Price of pattern, 7d. or 15 cts.

9675

9690   9690

No. 9690.—Boys' Suspender Trousers.—The pattern to these trousers is in 9 sizes for boys from 7 to 15 years of age. For a boy of 11 years, it will require 2⅛ yards of goods 27 inches wide. Price of pattern, 7d. or 15 cents.

9666   9666

No. 9666.—Misses' Coat.—At figure No. 296 elsewhere on this page, this coat is again seen. The pattern is in 8 sizes for misses from 8 to 15 years of age. For a miss of 13 years, it needs 5½ yards of goods 22 inches wide, or 2⅝ yards 48 inches wide. Price of pattern, 1s. or 25 cents.

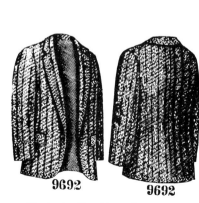

9692   9692

No. 9692.—Boys' Sack Coat, with Long Roll.—The pattern to this coat is in 9 sizes for boys from 7 to 15 years of age, and may be chosen for cloth of any variety. To make the garment for a boy of 11 years, will require 2⅛ yards of material 27 inches wide. Price of pattern, 10d. or 20 cents.

FIGURE No. 294.—GIRLS' STREET COSTUME.—This illustrates Girls' costume No. 9669, also shown on page 73. The pattern is in 8 sizes for girls from 5 to 12 years of age. For a girl of 8 years, it will require 5⅝ yards of material 22 inches wide, or 2⅝ yards 48 inches wide. Price of pattern, 1s. or 25 cents.

No. 9701.—BOYS' BICYCLE TROUSERS.—This pattern is in 9 sizes for boys from 7 to 15 years of age. To make the garment for a boy of 11 years, will require 1½ yard of material 27 inches wide, together with ¼ yard of stay linen 33 inches wide. Price of pattern, 7d. or 15 cents.

9701

9701

No. 9669.—GIRLS' STREET COSTUME. — Another illustration of this neat little costume is given at figure No. 294 on page 71 of this issue. The pattern is in 8 sizes for girls from 5 to 12 years of age. For a girl of 8 years, it needs 5⅝ yards of material 22 inches wide, or 2⅝ yards 48 inches wide. Price of pattern, 1s. or 25 cents.

9669

9669

9667

9667

No. 9667.—LADIES' COSTUME.—Another illustration of this elegant costume, showing a different combination of material and trimming, may be seen at figure No. 286 of this issue on page 69. The pattern is in 13 sizes for ladies from 28 to 46 inches, bust measure. To make the costume for a lady of medium size, requires 13½ yards of material 22 inches wide: the skirt needing 10¼ yards; and the basque, 3⅜ yards. If goods 48 inches wide be chosen, then 5⅝ yards will suffice for the skirt, and 1½ yard for the basque. Price of pattern, 1s. 6d. or 35 cents.

FIGURE No. 286.—LADIES' COSTUME.—This illustrates Ladies' costume No. 9667, again shown on page 73. Seal-brown Jersey cloth was here used for the basque, while the remainder of the costume is of twilled cloth, being trimmed with the same and bands of tinsel braid. The pattern is in 13 sizes for ladies from 28 to 46 inches, bust measure, and costs 1s. 6d. or 35 cents. For a lady of medium size, it needs 13½ yards of goods 22 inches wide.

No. 9672.—
LADIES' BASQUE.
—This pattern, al-
so shown at figure
No. 311 on page
74, is in 13 sizes
for ladies from 28
to 46 inches, bust
measure. For a
lady of medium
size, it needs $2\frac{7}{8}$
yards of plain ma-
terial and $\frac{5}{8}$ yard
of striped goods 22
inches wide, or $1\frac{1}{4}$
yard of plain and
$\frac{3}{8}$ yard of striped
48 inches wide.
Price of pattern,
1s. or 25 cents.

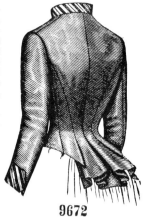

9672

9672

FIGURE No. 291.—LADIES' TOILETTE.—This consists of Ladies' basque No.
9706, again pictured on page 72 of this issue; and skirt No. 9705, portrayed in
a single material, with different trimming, on page 74. The pattern to the
basque is in 13 sizes for ladies from 28 to 46 inches, bust measure, and costs
1s. or 25 cents. The pattern to the skirt is in 9 sizes for ladies from 20 to 36
inches, waist measure, and costs 1s. 3d. or 30 cents. In making the costume of
a single material for a lady of medium size, $12\frac{5}{8}$ yards 22 inches wide will be
required; the basque calling for $2\frac{3}{4}$ yards, and the skirt for $9\frac{5}{8}$ yards. Of
goods 48 inches wide, the basque needs $1\frac{5}{8}$ yard; and the skirt, 5 yards.

No. 9673.—
LADIES' WALK-
ING SKIRT.—This
pattern, again
shown at figure
No. 311 on page
74, is in 9 sizes
for ladies from 20
to 36 inches, waist
measure. Cloth or
fashionable dress
goods will make
up stylishly in this
way, and braids or
other simple trim-
ming may be add-
ed. To make the
garment, without
the box - plaiting,
for a lady of medi-
um size, will need
$10\frac{3}{8}$ yards of material 22 inches
wide, or 5 yards
of goods 48 in-
ches wide. Price
of pattern, 1s.
3d. or 30 cents.

9673

9673

FIGURE No. 311.—LADIES' TOILETTE.—This consists
of Ladies' basque No. 9672, which is also shown on page
72; and skirt No. 9673, which is again seen on page
69. The basque pattern is in 13 sizes for ladies from 28
to 46 inches, bust measure, and costs 1s. or 25 cents. The
skirt pattern is in 9 sizes for ladies from 20 to 36 inches,
waist measure, and costs 1s. 3d. or 30 cents. For a lady
of medium size, it needs $13\frac{5}{8}$ yards of goods 22 inches wide.

No. 9706.—LADIES' BASQUE.—This basque is also prettily illustrated at figure No. 291 on page 70 of the present issue. The pattern is in 13 sizes for ladies from 28 to 46 inches, bust measure. To make the garment for a lady of medium size, will require 2¾ yards of material 22 inches wide, or 1¾ yard 36 inches wide, or 1⅜ yard 48 inches wide. Price of pattern, 1s. or 25 cents.

9706
9706

9705
9705

No. 9705.—LADIES' WALKING SKIRT.—A reference to figure No. 291 on page 70, shows this skirt developed in a similar variety of material, with another disposition of lace trimming. The pattern is in 9 sizes for ladies from 20 to 36 inches, waist measure. To make the garment for a lady of medium size, requires 9⅞ yards of material 22 inches wide, or 5⅞ yards 36 inches wide, or 5 yards 48 inches wide. Price of pattern, 1s. 3d. or 30 cents.

No. 9679.—LADIES' BASQUE, WITH ZOUAVE JACKET-FRONTS.—This pattern, also shown at figure No. 307 on page 73, is in 13 sizes for ladies from 28 to 46 inches, bust measure. For a lady of medium size, it needs 3¼ yards of one material and 1⅝ yard of another 22 inches wide, or 1½ yard of the one and ¾ yard of the other 48 ins. wide. Price, 1s. or 25 cents.

9679
9679

FIGURE NO. 307.—LADIES' TOILETTE.—This consists of Ladies' basque No. 9679, differently portrayed on page 72 of this issue; and skirt No. 9680, pictured in two views on page 74. The pattern to the basque is in 13 sizes for ladies from 28 to 46 inches, bust measure, and costs 1s. or 25 cents. The pattern to the skirt is in 9 sizes for ladies from 20 to 36 inches, waist measure, and costs 1s. 3d. or 30 cents. To make the costume of one material for a lady of medium size, will require 15¾ yards 22 inches wide; the basque calling for 4⅝ yards, and the skirt for 11¼ yards.

9680
9680

No. 9680.—LADIES' WALKING SKIRT.—This skirt is also represented at figure No. 307 on page 73. The pattern is in 9 sizes for ladies from 20 to 36 inches, waist measure, and is adapted to all varieties of dress goods. For a lady of medium size, it requires 11¼ yards of material 22 inches wide, or 5⅞ yards 48 inches wide, each with 6⅝ yards of velvet ribbon 2½ inches wide for the straps. Price of pattern, 1s. 3d. or 30 cents.

9702   **9702**

No. 9702.—BOYS' BLOUSE.—This pattern is in 8 sizes for boys from 3 to 10 years of age, and is suitable for flannels, serges, etc. To make the blouse for a boy of 7 years, will require 2⅛ yards of material 27 inches wide. Price of pattern, 10d. or 20 cents.

9707

No. 9707.—CHILD'S DRAWERS. — These drawers are made of fine muslin and trimmed with tucks and lace edging. The pattern is in 6 sizes for children from 1 to 6 years of age, and may be employed for all varieties of material adapted to such garments. To make the garment for a child of 6 years, will require ⅞ yard of material 36 inches wide. Price of pattern, 5d. or 10 cents.

9685   **9685**

No. 9685.—CHILD'S DRESS.–This pattern, again seen at figure No. 293 on page 70, is in 7 sizes for children from 6 months to 6 years old. For a child of 6 years, it needs 1 yard of goods 36 ins. wide, with 1¾ yard of flouncing 6½ ins. wide, and 2⅝ yards of flouncing 11½ ins. wide. Price, 7d. or 15 cts.

FIGURE No. 293.— CHILD'S DRESS.— This illustrates Child's dress No. 9685, shown in another material, with a different finish, on page 68. The pattern is in 7 sizes for children from 6 months to 6 years of age. For a child of 6 years, it needs 2⅝ yards of material 22 inches wide, or 1⅝ yard 36 inches wide, or 1⅛ yard 48 inches wide. Price of pattern, 7d. or 15 cents.

9678

No. 9678.—LADIES' SLEEVELESS ZOUAVE JACKET.—This pattern, again shown at figure No. 306 on page 73, is in 13 sizes for ladies from 28 to 46 inches, bust measure. For a lady of medium size, it needs 1¼ yard of material 22 inches wide. Price of pattern, 7d. or 15 cents.

9678

FIGURE No. 306.—LADIES' TOILETTE.—This consists of Ladies' polonaise No. 9681, again shown on page 71; jacket No. 9678, pictured in two views on page 74; and skirt No. 8682, differently portrayed on page 28 of this issue. The polonaise and jacket patterns are each in 13 sizes for ladies from 28 to 46 inches, bust measure: the polonaise costing 1s. 3d. or 30 cents; and the jacket, 7d. or 15 cents. The skirt pattern is in 9 sizes for ladies from 20 to 36 inches, waist measure, and costs 1s. 3d. or 30 cents.

9681

No. 9681. — LADIES' POLONAISE. —This garment is also illustrated at figure No. 306 on page 73. It is here represented as made of plain gingham, with embroidery for decoration. The pattern is in 13 sizes for ladies from 28 to 46 inches, bust measure, and may be employed for cashmeres, camel's-hairs, silks, woolens or any other variety of dress goods at present in vogue, with any trimming desirable. To make the garment for a lady of medium size, will require 7⅞ yards of material 22 inches wide, or 6 yards 36 inches wide. If goods 48 inches wide be selected, 3⅞ yards will be sufficient. Price of pattern, 1s. 3d. or 30 cts.

9681

9876   **9876**

No. 9876.—GIRLS' TRAVELLING WRAP. —By referring to figure No. 391 on page 91 of this issue, another view of this wrap may be seen. The pattern is in 7 sizes for girls from 3 to 9 years of age. For a girl of 8 years, it needs 4⅝ yards of material 22 inches wide, or 3⅝ yards 27 inches wide. If goods 48 inches wide be selected, 1⅞ yard will suffice. Price of pattern, 1s. or 25 cts.

9694   **9694**

No. 9694.—BOYS' BOX-PLAITED JACKET.— This jacket is again shown at figure No. 308 elsewhere on this page. The pattern is in 8 sizes for boys from 3 to 10 years old. For a boy of 7 years, it needs 2¼ yards of goods 27 inches wide. Price of pattern, 10d. or 20 cents.

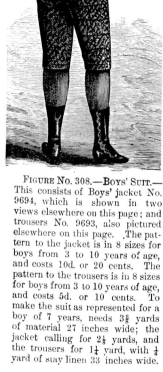

FIGURE NO. 308.—BOYS' SUIT.— This consists of Boys' jacket No. 9694, which is shown in two views elsewhere on this page; and trousers No. 9693, also pictured elsewhere on this page. The pattern to the jacket is in 8 sizes for boys from 3 to 10 years of age, and costs 10d. or 20 cents. The pattern to the trousers is in 8 sizes for boys from 3 to 10 years of age, and costs 5d. or 10 cents. To make the suit as represented for a boy of 7 years, needs 3⅝ yards of material 27 inches wide; the jacket calling for 2¼ yards, and the trousers for 1¼ yard, with ¼ yard of stay linen 33 inches wide.

9699   **9699**

No. 9699.—BOYS' JACKET, WITH SIMULATED VEST.—This pattern, shown at figure No. 287 on page 69, is in 8 sizes for boys from 5 to 12 years old. For a boy of 9 years, it requires 2¼ yards of goods 27 inches wide. Price of pattern, 10d. or 20 cents.

9696   **9696**

No. 9696.—BOYS' TROUSERS, EX-TENDING A LITTLE BELOW THE KNEE. —This pattern, again shown at figure No. 287 on page 69, is in 8 sizes for boys from 5 to 12 years of age. Price of pattern, 7d. or 15 cents.

FIGURE NO. 287.—BOYS' SUIT.—This consists of Boys' trousers No. 9696, pictured in two views on page 73; and jacket No. 9699, illustrated on page 71. The pattern to the trousers is in 8 sizes for boys from 5 to 12 years of age, and costs 7d. or 15 cents. The pattern to the jacket is in 8 sizes for boys from 5 to 12 years of age, and costs 10d. or 20 cents. To make the costume for a boy of 9 years, will require 3¾ yards of material 27 inches wide, with ¼ yard of stay linen.

FIGURE NO. 310.—BOYS' SUIT.— This consists of Boys' coat No. 9689, and trousers No. 9693, both of which are shown again else-where on this page. The material here illustrated is plain diagonal cloth, and braid binding and but-tons provide the tasteful finish. The coat pattern is in 8 sizes for boys from 3 to 10 years of age, and costs 10d. or 20 cents. The trousers pattern is in 8 sizes for boys from 3 to 10 years of age, and costs 5d. or 10 cents. To make the suit for a boy of 7 years, needs 3¼ yards of goods 27 inches wide; the coat calling for 1⅞ yard, and the trousers for 1¼ yard, with ¼ yard of stay linen 33 inches wide.

9689

No. 9689.—BOYS SACK COAT.— Another view of this coat is given at figure No. 310 else-where on this page. The pattern is in 8 sizes for boys from 3 to 10 years of age. To make the gar-ment for a boy of 7 years, will require 1¾ yard of material 27 inch-es wide. Price of pat-tern, 10d. or 20 cents.

9689

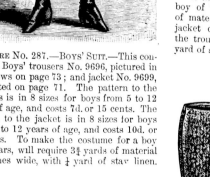

9693   **9693**

No. 9693.—BOYS' KNEE TROU-SERS, WITHOUT A FLY.—This pat-tern, again shown at figures Nos. 308 and 310 elsewhere on this page, is in 8 sizes for boys from 3 to 10 years of age. For a boy of 7 years, it will require 1¼ yard of material 27 inches wide. Price of pattern, **5d. or 10 cents.**

FIGURE No. 300.—BOYS' COSTUME.—This is Boys' skirt No. 9703, shown on page 68; and jacket No. 9704, pictured on page 73. Both are in 5 sizes for boys from 3 to 7 years of age, and each costs 7d. or 15 cents. For a boy of 6 years, they need 4¾ yards 27 inches wide.

9703   9703

No. 9703.—BOYS' BOX-PLAITED SKIRT, WITH SUPPORTING WAIST.—This pattern, again shown at figure No. 300 on page 71, is in 5 sizes for boys from 3 to 7 years old. For a boy of 6 years, it needs 1⅜ yard of goods 27 inches wide, with ⅝ yard of Silesia 36 inches wide. Price, 7d. or 15 cents.

9704   9704

No. 9704. — BOYS' DOUBLE-BREASTED JACKET.—This pattern, also seen at figure No. 300 on page 71, is in 5 sizes for boys from 3 to 7 years old. For a boy of 6 years, it needs 2 yards of material 27 inches wide, with 1 yard of contrasting goods in the same width. Price, 7d. or 15 cents.

No. 9710.— GIRLS' DRESS.— These engravings illustrate a pretty style of dress for a girl. The pattern is in 8 sizes for girls from 5 to 12 years of age, and is here used for Middlesex flannel, trimmed with silver braid. For a girl of 8 years, it needs 4¾ yards of material 22 inches wide, or 2⅝ yards 48 inches wide. Price of pattern, 10d. or 20 cents.

9710   9710

FIGURE No. 297.—GIRLS' COSTUME.—This illustrates Girls' costume No. 9708, which is again pictured on page 72 of this issue. The pattern is in 8 sizes for girls from 5 to 12 years of age, and costs 1s. or 25 cents. To make the costume of one material for a girl of 8 years, needs 6 yards 22 inches wide, or 2⅝ yards 48 inches wide.

No. 9700.—BOYS' BICYCLE BLOUSE.— This pattern is in 9 sizes for boys from 7 to 15 years of age, and may be developed in all varieties of seasonable fabrics. To make the blouse for a boy of 11 years, will require 3¼ yards of material 27 inches wide. Price of pattern, 10d. or 20 cents.

9700   9700

No. 9708.— GIRLS' COSTUME. —This costume is also shown at figure No. 297 on page 71. The pattern is in 8 sizes for girls from 5 to 12 years of age. For a girl of 8 years, it needs 5 yards of goods 22 inches wide, with 1 yard of Surah 20 inches wide for the vest and scarf. Price, 1s. or 25 cents.

9708   9708

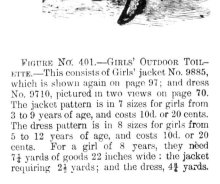

FIGURE No. 401.—GIRLS' OUTDOOR TOILETTE.—This consists of Girls' jacket No. 9885, which is shown again on page 97; and dress No. 9710, pictured in two views on page 70. The jacket pattern is in 7 sizes for girls from 3 to 9 years of age, and costs 10d. or 20 cents. The dress pattern is in 8 sizes for girls from 5 to 12 years of age, and costs 10d. or 20 cents. For a girl of 8 years, they need 7¼ yards of goods 22 inches wide : the jacket requiring 2¼ yards; and the dress, 4¾ yards.

No. 9718.—CHILD'S UNDER-DRESS.—This little pattern is in 7 sizes for children from 6 months to 6 years of age. For a child of 4 years, it needs 1⅝ yard of goods 27 inches wide, or 1¼ yard 36 inches wide. Price of pattern, 7d. or 15 cts.

9718

9718

No. 9712.—LADIES' WALKING SKIRT.—Another view of this skirt is given at figure No. 299 on page 71. Plain gray cloth, with fancy braid for trimming, was here employed for it. The pattern is in 9 sizes for ladies from 20 to 36 inches, waist measure. For a lady of medium size, it will require 9⅞ yards of material 22 inches wide, or 5⅝ yards of goods 48 inches wide. Price of pattern, 1s. 3d. or 30 cents.

9712

9712

No. 9713.—LADIES' BASQUE.—Another view of this garment may be seen by referring to figure No. 299 on page 71 of this issue. The pattern is in 13 sizes for ladies from 28 to 46 inches, bust measure. To make the garment for a lady of medium size, requires 3⅝ yards of material 22 inches wide, or 1¾ yard 48 inches wide. Price of pattern, 1s. or 25 cents.

9713

9713

No. 9715.—LADIES' JACKET.—This pattern is in 13 sizes for ladies from 28 to 46 inches, bust measure, and is charming for coatings and suitings of all kinds. To make the garment for a lady of medium size, will require 4⅝ yards of material 22 inches wide, or 2¼ yards 48 inches wide. Price of pattern, 1s. 3d. or 30 cents.

9715

9715

FIGURE NO. 299.—LADIES' MOURNING TOILETTE.—This consists of Ladies' walking skirt No. 9712, two views of which are given on page 70; and basque No. 9713, which is differently portrayed on page 70. The skirt pattern is in 9 sizes for ladies from 20 to 36 inches, waist measure, and costs 1s. 3d. or 30 cents. The basque pattern is in 13 sizes for ladies from 28 to 46 inches, bust measure, and costs 1s. or 25 cents. For a lady of medium size, they need 13½ yards of goods 22 inches wide: the skirt requiring 9⅞ yards; and the basque, 3⅝ yards.

No. 9716.—LA-
DIES' PLAITED
BASQUE.—This
pattern is in 13
sizes for ladies
from 28 to 46 in-
ches, bust meas-
ure, and will de-
velop stylishly in
any variety of
dress goods. To
make the basque
for a lady of me-
dium size, needs 4⅝
yards of material
22 inches wide, or
2⅝ yards 36 inch-
es wide, or 2 yards
48 inches wide.
Price of pattern,
1s. or 25 cents.

9716

9716

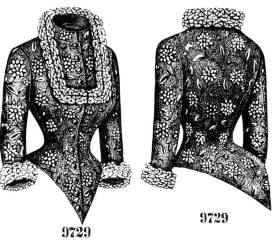

9729

9729

No. 9729.—LADIES' POINTED BASQUE.—Plain and brocaded silk are here illustrated, the plain silk being applied
in the form of ruching. The pattern is in 13 sizes for ladies
from 28 to 46 inches, bust measure. For a lady of medium size, it requires 2⅞ yards of material 22 inches wide,
or 1⅜ yard 48 inches wide. Price of pattern, 1s. or 25 cents.

9719

9719

No. 9719.—INFANTS' DRESS, WITH SEAMLESS,
POINTED YOKE.—Nainsook and lace net are combined in this pretty dress, lace and tucks being
used for decoration. Any other preferred variety of goods may, however, be chosen, and the
garment may be completed as elaborately as desired. The pattern is in one size, and, to make a
dress like it, requires 2¼ yards of material 36 inches wide, with ⅝ yard of lace net 21 inches wide
for the yoke. Price of pattern, 7d. or 15 cents.

9714

9714

No. 9714.—LADIES' TRAINED COSTUME.—
Plain and brocaded silk were employed for
the construction of this handsome costume,
lace trimming it very elaborately. The pattern is in 13 sizes for ladies from 28 to 46
inches, bust measure. For a lady of medium
size, it requires 8½ yards of plain goods for
the skirt, and 9⅝ yards of brocaded material
for the over-dress, each 22 inches wide; or 4
yards of the one and 4⅝ yards of the other 48
inches wide. Price of pattern, 2s. or 50 cents.

No. 9722.— GIRLS' COSTUME.—This pattern, again shown at figure No. 336 on page 79, is in 7 sizes for girls from 3 to 9 years of age. For a girl of 8 years, it needs 4⅞ yds. of goods 22 ins. wide, or 2⅞ yds. 36 ins. wide, with ⅝ yard of Silesia 36 ins. wide for the waist. Price, 10d. or 20 cents.

9722

9722

No. 9721.— CHILD'S COSTUME. —This pattern, also seen at figure No. 333 on page 78, is in 6 sizes for children from 1 to 6 years of age. For a child of 4 years, it needs 2¼ yards of figured and ½ yard of plain goods, each 22 inches wide, or 1⅜ yard of the one and ⅜ yard of the other 36 inches wide. Price of pattern, 7d. or 15 cents.

9721

9721

FIGURE NO. 333.—CHILD'S COSTUME.—This illustrates Child's costume No. 9721, again shown on page 79 of this issue. The pattern is in 6 sizes for children from 1 to 6 years of age, and costs 7d. or 15 cents. For a child of 4 years, it needs 2⅝ yards of goods 22 inches wide.

FIGURE NO. 336.—GIRLS' COSTUME.—This illustrates Girls' costume No. 9722, also shown on page 78. Plain and plaid flannel are combined in the present instance, the disposal of the two being especially effective. The pattern is in 7 sizes for girls from 3 to 9 years of age. To make the costume for a girl of 8 years, will require 4⅞ yards of material 22 inches wide, with ⅝ yard of Silesia 36 inches wide for the waist. Price of pattern, 10d. or 20 cents.

No. 9720.— MISSES' COSTUME.—This costume is shown in a different combination of materials and trimmings at figure No. 320 on page 76. The pattern is in 8 sizes for misses from 8 to 15 years of age, and is adapted to all varieties of dress goods in vogue. For a miss of 13 years, it requires 8½ yards of material 22 inches wide, or 4⅔ yards 48 inches wide, each with 1¼ yard of velvet 20 inches wide for the vest, collar and bands. Price of pattern, 1s. 3d. or 30 cents.

FIGURE NO. 320.—MISSES' COSTUME.—This illustrates Misses' costume No. 9720, again shown on page 77. The pattern is in 8 sizes for misses from 8 to 15 years of age. Without the box-plaited trimming, for a miss of 13 years, it will require 8½ yards of material 22 inches wide, or 4⅔ yards 48 inches wide, each with 1¼ yard of velvet 20 inches wide. Price of pattern, 1s. 3d. or 30 cents.

9720

9720

No. 9914.—
GIRLS' COSTUME.
—This costume
isagam illustrat-
ed at figure No.
409 on page 95.
The pattern is in
7 sizes for girls
from 3 to 9 years
of age. For a
girl of 8 years, it
needs 4⅞ yards
of materi 1 22
inches wide, or
2¼ yards 48 inch-
es wide. Price
of pattern, 1s.
or 25 cents.

9914

9914

No. 9727—
MISSES' COS-
TUME.—G r a y
cashmere w a s
employed for the
costume here il-
lustrated, and
the skirt is fin-
ished with a nar-
row box-plaiting
of the same.
Braid arranged
in a fanciful man-
ner is also used
for decoration.
The pattern is in
8 sizes for misses
from 8 to 15
years of age. To
make the
costume for a
miss of 13 years,
will require 10⅝
yards of material
22 inches wide,
or 5 yards of
goods 48 inches
wide. Price of
pattern, 1s. 3d.
or 30 cents.

9727

9727

No. 9890.—LADIES' APRON.—Cross-barred nainscok was
the fabric chosen for the formation of the apron pictured
in the above engraving, and lace and insertion form the
trimming. It is a very pretty design, and is fitted over
the hips by darts. The pattern is in one size, and, to make
an apron like it, needs 1¼ yard of material 22 inches wide,
or 1⅛ yard 36 inches wide. Price of pattern, 7d. or 15 cents.

9890

9723

9723

FIGURE NO. 324.—LADIES' COSTUME.—This illustrates
Ladies' costume No. 9723, two views of which are given on
page 75 of this issue. Light-weight cloth was chosen for
the costume in the present instance, and the material, facings of silk and tinsel braid form the trimming. The pattern is in 13 sizes for ladies from 28 to 46 inches, bust measure. To make the costume for a lady of medium size, will require 11¾ yards of material 22 inches wide, or 5¼ yards of
goods 48 inches wide. Price of pattern, 1s. 6d. or 35 cents.

No. 9723.—LADIES' COSTUME.—At figure No. 324 on page 77, another
illustration of this stylish garment may be seen. The pattern is in 13 sizes
for ladies from 28 to 46 inches, bust measure, and is here employed for
cashmere, with the same and velvet for decoration. To make the costume
for a lady of medium size, will require 11¾ yards of material 22 inches
wide, or 5½ yards 48 inches wide. Price of pattern, 1s. 6d. or 35 cents.

No. 9726.—LADIES' POLONAISE.— This pattern is in 13 sizes for ladies from 28 to 46 inches, bust measure. Figured cashmere was chosen for the garment in the present instance, and buttons provide the only decoration. Lace, embroidery, braid or any other preferred style of trimming may, however, be added to the edges, with very pretty results. To make the polonaise for a lady of medium size, will require 8⅝ yards of material 22 inches wide, or 5⅝ yards 36 inches wide, or 4¼ yards 48 inches wide. Price of pattern, 1s. 3d. or 30 cents.

9726

9726

FIGURE No. 321.—LADIES' COSTUME.—This illustrates Ladies' costume No. 9724, which is shown in another material, with braid for decoration, elsewhere on this page. Surah silk was here employed for the costume, with plaitings of the same and tiny silk crochetted buttons for trimming. The pattern is in 13 sizes for ladies from 28 to 46 inches, bust measure, and may be chosen for any fashionable suiting. To make the costume for a lady of medium size, will require 13 yards of material 22 inches wide, or 6¼ yards of goods 48 inches wide. Price of pattern, 1s. 6d. or 35 cents.

9724

9724

No. 9724.—LADIES' COSTUME.—Another view of this costume is given at figure No. 321 elsewhere on this page. Cashmere was employed for the garment in this instance, with knife-plaitings of the same and braid for decoration. The pattern is in 13 sizes for ladies from 28 to 46 inches, bust measure. To make the costume for a lady of medium size, requires 13 yards of material 22 inches wide, or 6¼ yards 48 inches wide. Price of pattern, 1s. 6d. or 35 cents.

FIGURE No. 338.—CHILD'S DRESS.—This illustrates Child's dress No. 9730, pictured in different material elsewhere on this page. The pattern is in 7 sizes for children from 6 months to 6 years of age, and costs 7d. or 15 cents. For a child of 4 years, it needs 1⅞ yard of material 22 inches wide, or 1½ yard 36 inches wide.

No. 9730.—CHILD'S DRESS.—This pattern, again pictured at figure No. 338 elsewhere on this page, is in 7 sizes for children from 6 months to 6 years of age. For a child of 4 years, it needs 1⅞ yard of material 22 inches wide, or 1½ yard 36 inches wide, or ⅞ yard 48 inches wide. Price, 7d. or 15 cents.

9730

9730

9753 **9753**

No. 9753.—BOYS' SAILOR BLOUSE-WAIST.—This pattern is in 10 sizes for boys from 3 to 12 years of age. To make the waist for a boy of 7 years, will require 2 yards of material 27 inches wide. Price of pattern, 10d. or 20 cents.

No. 9734.—LADIES' BASQUE.—This pattern, again shown at figure No. 319 on page 76, is in 13 sizes for ladies from 28 to 46 inches, bust measure. For a lady of medium size, it needs 3⅓ yards of material 22 inches wide, or 1½ yard 48 inches wide. Price of pattern, 1s. or 25 cents.

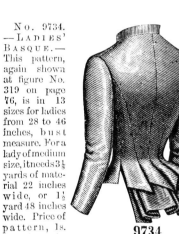

9734 **9734**

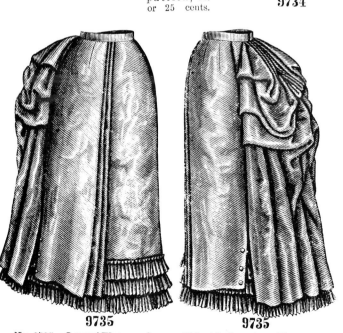

9735 **9735**

No. 9735.—LADIES' WALKING SKIRT.—This skirt is portrayed in a combination of plain and flowered foulard at figure No. 319 on page 76 of this issue. It is here made of plain suit goods, and trimmed with three knife-plaitings of the same and buttons. The pattern is in 9 sizes for ladies from 20 to 36 inches, waist measure. To make the garment for a lady of medium size, will require 10¼ yards of material 22 inches wide, or 4⅞ yards 48 inches wide. Price of pattern, 1s. 3d. or 30 cents.

FIGURE No. 319.—LADIES' TOILETTE.—This consists of Ladies' basque No. 9734, which is differently illustrated on page 75; and skirt No. 9735, two views of which are given on page 79. The pattern to the basque is in 13 sizes for ladies from 28 to 46 inches, bust measure, and costs 1s. or 25 cents. The pattern to the skirt is in 9 sizes for ladies from 20 to 36 inches, waist measure, and costs 1s. 3d. or 30 cents. To make the toilette of one material for a lady of medium size, requires 13⅞ yards 22 inches wide: the skirt needing 10¼ yards; and the basque, 3⅓ yards. If goods 48 inches wide be chosen, then 4⅞ yards will suffice for the skirt, and 1½ yard for the basque.

No. 9728.—
Misses' Jack-
et.— Another
view of this
jacket is given
at figure No.
340 on page
79 of the pres-
ent issue. The
pattern is in 8
sizes for miss-
es from 8 to
15 years of
age. To make
the garment
for a miss of
13 years, will
require 4¼
yards of ma-
terial 22 inches wide, or 3⅝ yards 27 inches wide, or 1⅞ yard
48 inches wide. Price of pattern, 10d. or 20 cents.

9728   **9728**

FIGURE No. 322.—Girls' Costume.
—This illustrates Girls' costume No.
9739, again shown on page 75 of this
issue. The pattern is in 7 sizes for
girls from 3 to 9 years of age, and
may be developed in any suitable
fabric. To make the costume as represented for a girl of 8 years, will require 1¾ yard of Jersey cloth 27 inches
wide for the basque, and 2¾ yards of
plaid goods 22 inches wide for the skirt.
Price of pattern, 10d. or 20 cents.

9739

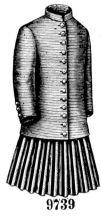

No. 9739.—
Girls' Costume.
—At figure No.
322 on page 76,
this costume
may again be
seen. The pat-
tern is in 7 sizes
for girls from 3
to 9 years of age.
For a girl of 8
years, it needs 2¾
yards of striped
goods 22 inches
wide, with 1¾
yard of Jersey
cloth 27 inches
wide. Price,
10d. or 20 cents.

9739

FIGURE No. 340.—Misses' Street Costume.—
This consists of Misses' jacket No. 9728, which is
differently illustrated on page 75 of this issue; and
box-plaited skirt No. 8418, again pictured on
page 46. Both patterns are in 8 sizes for misses
from 8 to 15 years of age: the jacket costing
10d. or 20 cents; and the skirt, 1s. 3d. or 30 cents
To make the costume for a miss of 13 years,
requires 9¼ yards of goods 22 inches wide: the
skirt needing 4⅞ yards; and the jacket, 4¼ yards.

No. 9748.—Infants' Flannel
Band.—Soft white flannel was
employed for this band, with
feather-stitching for finishing the
hems. The pattern is in one
size, and, to make a band like it,
will require ¼ yard of goods 27 inches wide. Price, 3d. or 5 cents.

9748

9711   **9711**

No. 9711.—Child's Jacket.—The pattern to this little jacket is in 6 sizes for
children from 1 to 6 years of age.
For a child of 6 years, it will require
2¼ yards of material 22 inches wide,
or 2 yards 27 inches wide, or 1 yard
48 inches wide. Price, 7d. or 15 cents.

9738   **9738**

No. 9738.—Infants' Wrapper.—Figured cashmere was used for the pretty wrapper here pictured. Ribbon bows and fancy stitching provide
the decorations in this instance, but any other
style of finish admired may be chosen. The pattern is in one size, and, to make the garment as
here represented, will require 3¼ yards of material
22 inches wide, or 2⅞ yards 27 inches wide. If
goods 36 inches wide be used, 2¼ yards will be
sufficient. Price of pattern, 7d. or 15 cents.

9732　　　　　　　　　　　**9732**

No. 9732.— CHILD'S COS-TUME.—The pattern to this costume is in 6 sizes for children from 1 to 6 years of age. For a child of 4 years, it requires 2¾ yards of goods 22 inches wide, or 1⅜ yard 48 inches wide, each with ⅜ yard of velvet 20 inches wide. Price of pattern, 7d. or 15 cents.

9834

No. 9834.— GIRLS' COSTUME. —This costume is pictured in another material and with other decorations at figure No. 374 on page 87 of this issue. The pattern is in 7 sizes for girls from 3 to 9 years of age. To make the costume for a girl of 8 years, will require 3⅞ yards of material 22 inches wide, or 1½ yard 48 inches wide. Price of pattern, 1s. or 25 cts.

9834

9737　　　　　　　**9737**

No. 9737.—MISSES' COSTUME.—The above engravings represent a pretty costume of figured dress goods. The mode is very stylish and will be much used for washable goods. The pattern is in 8 sizes for misses from 8 to 15 years of age. To make the costume for a miss of 13 years, will require 10⅝ yards of material 22 inches wide, or 8¼ yards 36 inches wide, or 5⅛ yards 48 inches wide. Price of pattern, 1s. 3d. or 30 cents.

9740　　　　　　　　　**9740**

FIGURE No. 327.—LADIES' COSTUME.—This illustrates Ladies' costume No. 9740, also represented on page 75. Velvet and cloth are here combined, with velvet and *passementerie*-ornaments for decorations. The pattern is in 13 sizes for ladies from 28 to 46 inches, bust measure, and may be selected for any variety of dress goods at present in vogue. To make the costume of one material for a lady of medium size, will require 16¼ yards 22 inches wide, or 7¾ yards 48 inches wide. Price of pattern, 1s. 6d. or 35 cents.

No. 9740.—LADIES' COSTUME.—At figure No. 327 on page 77 of the present issue, may be seen another view of this costume. The pattern is in 13 sizes for ladies from 28 to 46 inches, bust measure. To make the garment for a lady of medium size, will require 16¼ yards of material 22 inches wide, or 7¾ yards of goods 48 inches wide, each with 1¼ yard of velvet 20 inches wide for the collar, panels, laps and facings. Price of pattern, 1s. 6d. or 35 cents.

9756

9756

No. 9760.—
MISSES'AND CHIL-
DREN'S COLLAR.—
This pattern is in
3 sizes—11, 13
and 15 inches,

9760

neck measures. A collar measuring
13 inches, needs ⅞ yard of embroidery
5¾ inches deep, with 1⅛ yard of the
same 2¾ inches deep, and ½ yard of
nainsook. Price of pattern, 3d. or 5 cts.

No. 9761.—LADIES'
NIGHT-CAP.—This pat-
tern is in one size, and
may be employed for
any variety of mate-
rial suitable for such
caps. In making a
cap like the one here
illustrated, ⅝ yard of
material 36 inches
wide will be re-
quired. Price of pat-
tern, 5d. or 10 cents.

9761

No. 9756.—LADIES' WRAP.—Brocaded velvet was used for the
stylish wrap here pictured, with lace and *passementerie* for decoration. The pattern is in 10 sizes for ladies from 28 to 46 inches,
bust measure. For a lady of medium size, it will require 3⅜
yards of material 22 inches wide, or 1½ yard 48 inches wide, or
1½ yard 54 inches wide. Price of pattern, 1s. or 25 cents.

9743

FIGURE NO. 334.—GIRLS' STREET TOILETTE.—This
consists of Girls' jacket No. 9743, also shown on page
77; and costume No. 9106, pictured on page 43.
The jacket pattern is in 7 sizes for girls from 3 to 9
years of age, and costs 7d. or 15 cents. The costume
pattern is in 7 sizes for girls from 3 to 9 years of age,
and costs 10d. or 20 cents. For a girl of 8 years,
they require 9¼ yards of material 22 inches wide.

No. 9743.—GIRLS' JACKET.—This
pattern, again shown at figure No.
334 on page 79, is in 7 sizes for girls
from 3 to 9 years of age. For a girl
of 8 years, it needs 3 yards of goods
22 inches wide, or 1⅝ yard 48 inches
wide. Price of pattern, 7d. or 15 cts.

FIGURE NO. 326.—GIRLS' COSTUME.—This
illustrates Girls' costume No. 9741, which is
differently portrayed on page 78 of the present issue. The pattern is in 7 sizes for girls
from 3 to 9 years of age, and costs 10d. or
20 cents. To make the costume for a girl of 8
years, will require 6½ yards of material 22 inches wide, or 3⅜ yards of goods 48 inches wide.

9741

No. 9741.—
GIRLS' COS-
TUME.—This
costume is
again shown in
figure No. 326
on page 77.
The pattern is
in 7 sizes for
girls from 3 to
9 years of age.
For a girl of 8
years, it needs
6½ yards of ma-
terial 22 inches
wide, or 3½
yards 36 inch-
es wide. Price
of pattern, 10d.
or 20 cents.

9741

9754   **9754**

NO. 9754.—BOYS' OVER-
ALLS.—This pattern is in
11 sizes for boys from 5
to 15 years of age. For a
boy of 9 years, it needs 2⅛
yards of goods 27 inches
wide. Price, 7d. or 15 cts.

49

No. 9717.—Misses' Box-Plaited Blouse.—Another illustration of this garment is given at figure No. 337 on page 79 of this publication. The pattern is in 8 sizes for misses from 8 to 15 years of age. For a miss of 13 years, it will require 4 yards of material 22 inches wide, or 2⅝ yards 36 inches wide, or 1⅞ yard 48 inches wide. Price of pattern, 10d. or 20 cents.

9717

9717

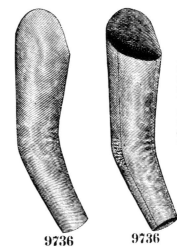

No. 9736.—Ladies' Sleeve, Gathered at the Elbow.—In ordering the pattern, the size the sleeve is desired to be around the muscular part of the upper arm should be given. The pattern is in 3 sizes—11, 13 and 15 inches. For a pair of sleeves measuring 13 inches as mentioned, it needs 1¼ yard of material 22 inches wide, or ⅝ yard either 36, 48 or 54 inches wide. Price of pattern, 5d. or 10 cents.

9736   **9736**

Figure No. 337.—Misses' Toilette.—This consists of Misses' blouse No. 9717, also shown on page 77; and walking skirt No. 9744, again pictured on page 76. Navy-blue flannel was employed for the garments in this instance, with facings of crimson silk, fancy stitching and a plaiting of the goods for trimming. Both patterns are in 8 sizes for misses from 8 to 15 years of age: the blouse costing 10d. or 20 cents; and the skirt, 1s. or 25 cents. For a miss of 13 years, they require 11½ yards of material 22 inches wide: the blouse needing 4 yards: and the skirt, 7½ yards.

9762   **9762**

No. 9762.—Ladies' Wrap.—Brocaded Ottoman was employed for this stylish wrap, and lace provides the decoration. The pattern is in 10 sizes for ladies from 28 to 46 inches, bust measure. To make the wrap for a lady of medium size, will require 4 yards of material 22 inches wide, or 1¾ yard 48 inches wide, or 1⅝ yard 54 inches wide, each with 4⅛ yards of silk 20 inches wide for lining. Price of pattern, 1s. or 25 cents.

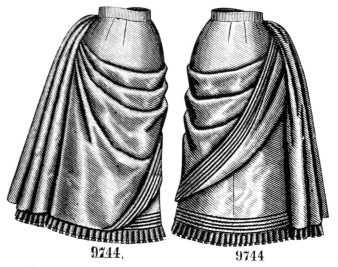

9744   **9744**

No. 9744.—Misses' Walking Skirt.—Another view of this skirt is given at figure No. 337 on page 79. Plain dress goods were employed for the garment in the present instance, with a plaiting and facing of the material and narrow braid for trimming. The pattern is in 8 sizes for misses from 8 to 15 years of age. To make the skirt for a miss of 13 years, needs 7½ yards of material 22 inches wide, or 3½ yards 48 inches wide. Price of pattern, 1s. or 25 cents.

9767   **9767**

No. 9767.—LADIES' COAT.—This coat is made of plain cloth, buttons and simulated button-holes giving a neat finish. The pattern is in 13 sizes for ladies from 28 to 46 inches, bust measure. For a lady of medium size, it needs 4¾ yards of goods 22 inches wide, or 1⅞ yard 48 inches wide, or 1¾ yard 54 inches wide. Price, 1s. 3d. or 30 cents.

No. 9768.—LADIES' COAT.—The jaunty garment here portrayed is made of cloth and trimmed with rows of fine braid. The pattern is in 13 sizes for ladies from 28 to 46 inches, bust measure, and may be chosen for any variety of Spring coating desired. To make the coat for a lady of medium size, will require 4½ yards of material 22 inches wide, or 2¼ yards 48 inches wide. If goods 54 inches wide be selected, then 1⅝ yard will be sufficient. Price of pattern, 1s. 3d. or 30 cents.

9768   **9768**

No. 9746.—MISSES' BASQUE.—At figure No. 328 elsewhere on this page, another view of this basque is given. The pattern is in 8 sizes for misses from 8 to 15 years of age. To make the garment for a miss of 13 years, will require 3¼ yards of material 22 inches wide, or 1½ yard of goods 48 inches wide. Price of pattern, 10d. or 20 cents.

9746   **9746**

9745   **9745**

FIGURE NO. 328.—MISSES' TOILETTE.—This consists of Misses' basque No. 9746, shown again elsewhere on this page; and skirt No. 9745, also illustrated on page 76. Both patterns are in 8 sizes for misses from 8 to 15 years of age: the basque costing 10d. or 20 cents; and the skirt, 1s. or 25 cents. To make the toilette for a miss of 13 years, will require 10⅓ yards of material 22 inches wide.

No. 9745.—MISSES' WALKING SKIRT.—This skirt is differently represented at figure No. 328 on page 77. Plain suiting is here represented, and a plaiting of the material and narrow braid constitute the garnitures. The pattern is in 8 sizes for misses from 8 to 15 years of age. For a miss of 13 years, it needs 7 yards of material 22 ins. wide, or 3¾ yards 48 inches wide. Price of pattern, 1s. or 25 cents.

9747

9747

No. 9747.—LADIES' WRAP.—This wrap is portrayed in different materials at figure No. 317 on page 75. The pattern is in 10 sizes for ladies from 28 to 46 inches, bust measure. To make the garment of one material for a lady of medium size, requires 4¼ yards 22 inches wide, or 1⅞ yard 48 inches wide, or 1¼ yard 54 inches wide. As here represented, it will need 2⅝ yards of plain goods and 2 yards of brocaded 22 inches wide. Price of pattern, 1s. or 25 cents.

9787

9787

No. 9787.—LADIES' WRAPPER.—Figured wash goods were employed for the construction of this wrapper, and a flounce of the material trims the lower portion of the skirt. The pattern is in 13 sizes for ladies from 28 to 46 inches, bust measure. To make the garment for a lady of medium size, requires 9⅝ yards of goods 22 inches wide, or 5¾ yards 36 inches wide, or 4¼ yards 48 inches wide. Price of pattern, 1s. 6d. or 35 cents.

9788

9788

FIGURE No. 317.—LADIES WRAP.—This illustrates Ladies wrap No. 9747, which is shown in a different combination of materials on page 79. In this instance velvet is used for the back and fronts, and Spanish lace net over crimson Surah for the sleeves, which fall considerably below the back and are gathered to stand high on the shoulders. The pattern is in 10 sizes for ladies from 28 to 46 inches, bust measure. To make the wrap of two kinds of material, each 22 inches wide, requires 2 yards for the sleeves and 2⅝ yards for the remainder. Of one fabric throughout, it needs 4⅛ yards 22 inches wide, or 1⅞ yard 48 inches wide, or 1¼ yard 54 inches wide. Price of pattern, 1s. or 25 cents.

No. 9788.—LADIES' WRAP.—This pattern is in 10 sizes for ladies from 28 to 46 inches, bust measure, and may be used for any variety of wrap material. To make the garment for a lady of medium size, will require 5 yards of goods 22 inches wide, or 2⅝ yards 48 inches wide, or 2⅝ yards 54 inches wide. Price of pattern, 1s. 3d. or 30 cents.

9733   **9733**

No. 9733.—Child's Apron. The pretty little apron here depicted is made of plaid cambric and trimmed with embroidery. Any appropriate fabric may, however, be used for it. The pattern is in 4 sizes for children from 6 months to 3 years of age. To make the apron for a child of 1 year, needs ⅝ yard of material 36 inches wide. Price of pattern, 5d. or 10 cts.

No. 9772. —Ladies' Basque.—This pattern is in 13 sizes for ladies from 28 to 46 inches, bust measure, and is adapted to cloth, cashmere, flannel, etc. For a lady of medium size, it needs 4 yards of goods 22 inches wide, or 1¾ yard 48 inches wide. Price of pattern, 1s. or 25 cents.

9772   **9772**

9749

9749

No. 9749.—Ladies' Basque.—Another view of this garment is given at figure No. 331 on page 78 of this issue. The pattern is in 13 sizes for ladies from 28 to 46 inches, bust measure. For a lady of medium size, it requires 3¾ yards of one material and ⅝ yard of contrasting goods 22 inches wide. Price of pattern, 1s. or 25 cents.

Figure No. 331.—Ladies' Toilette.—This consists of Ladies' skirt No. 9750, and basque No. 9749, both shown again on page 79. The skirt pattern is in 9 sizes for ladies from 20 to 36 inches, waist measure, and costs 1s. 3d. or 30 cents. The basque pattern is in 13 sizes for ladies from 28 to 46 inches, bust measure, and costs 1s. or 25 cents. For a lady of medium size, they need 15⅞ yards of goods 22 inches wide.

9750   **9750**

No. 9750.—Ladies' Walking Skirt.—Another illustration of this skirt is given at figure No. 331 on page 78 of this issue. The pattern is in 9 sizes for ladies from 20 to 36 inches, waist measure, and may be developed in a single variety of goods if preferred. To make the garment for a lady of medium size, will require 5½ yards of plain material and 6 yards of figured goods 22 inches wide, or 3½ yards of the one and 3 yards of the other 48 inches wide. Price of pattern, 1s. 3d. or 30 cents.

No. 9755.—
CHILD'S JACKET.--
This pattern, also
shown at figure
No. 339 on page
79, is in 6 sizes for
children from 1 to
6 years old. For a
child of 4 years, it
needs 2¼ yds. 22
inches wide, or 1
yd. 48 ins. wide,
each with ½ yd. of
velvet 20 in. wide.
Price, 7d. or 15 cts.

9755   **9755**

FIGURE NO. 339.—CHILD'S JACKET.—This
is Child's jacket No. 9755, shown in two views
on page 78. The pattern is in 6 sizes for children from 1 to 6 years of age. For a child
of 4 years, it needs 2¼ yards of goods 22 inches
wide, or 1¼ yard 27 inches wide, or 1 yard 48
inches wide. Price of pattern, 7d. or 15 cents.

9752

9752

No. 9752.—LADIES' BASQUE.—Another illustration of this garment may be observed by referring to figure No. 316 on page 75 of
this issue. Plain suit goods and velvet are pictured in the present
instance. The pattern is in 13 sizes for ladies from 28 to 46 inches,
bust measure. To make the garment for a lady of medium size, will
require 3¼ yards of material 22 inches wide. Of goods 48 inches
wide, 1⅝ yard will be sufficient. Price of pattern, 1s. or 25 cents.

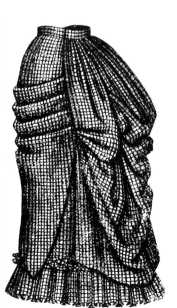

No. 9751.
—LADIES'
WALKING
SKIRT.—At
figure No. 316
on page 75,
this skirt is
shown in ano-
ther material
and with dif-
ferent decora-
tions. The pat-
tern is in 9
sizes for ladies
from 20 to 36
inches, waist
measure. For
a lady of me-
dium size, it
needs 9¾ yards
of material 22
inches wide, or
5⅞ yards 36 in-
ches wide, or
5 yards 48 in-
ches wide.
Price of pat-
tern, 1s. 3d.
or 30 cents.

9751   **9751**

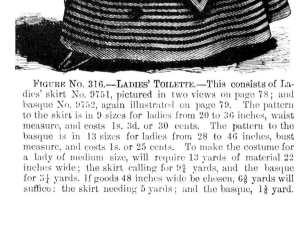

FIGURE NO. 316.—LADIES' TOILETTE.—This consists of Ladies' skirt No. 9751, pictured in two views on page 78; and
basque No. 9752, again illustrated on page 79. The pattern
to the skirt is in 9 sizes for ladies from 20 to 36 inches, waist
measure, and costs 1s. 3d. or 30 cents. The pattern to the
basque is in 13 sizes for ladies from 28 to 46 inches, bust
measure, and costs 1s. or 25 cents. To make the costume for
a lady of medium size, will require 13 yards of material 22
inches wide; the skirt calling for 9¾ yards, and the basque
for 3¼ yards. If goods 48 inches wide be chosen, 6⅝ yards will
suffice: the skirt needing 5 yards; and the basque, 1⅝ yard.

9791   **9791**

No. 9791.—Misses' Blouse Costume.—This pattern is in 8 sizes for misses from 8 to 15 years of age. For a miss of 13 years, it needs 3¼ yards of dark material and 7¾ yards of light goods 22 inches wide, or 2¼ yards of the one and 6½ yards of the other 36 inches wide. Price of pattern, 1s. 3d. or 30 cents.

9789   **9789**

No. 9789.—Ladies' Coat, with Full Skirt.—This pattern is in 13 sizes for ladies from 28 to 46 inches, bust measure. For a lady of medium size, it needs 7¾ yards of material 22 inches wide, or 3¾ yards 48 inches wide, or 3⅝ yards 54 inches wide. Price of pattern, 1s. 3d. or 30 cents.

Figure No. 330.—Misses' Sack Apron.—This illustrates Misses' apron No. 9757, which is portrayed in a different combination of material and decoration on page 77 of this issue. The pattern is in 8 sizes for misses from 8 to 15 years of age, and costs 10d. or 20 cents. To make the apron for a miss of 13 years, will require 2¾ yards of material 36 inches wide.

9757   **9757**

No. 9757.—Misses' Sack Apron.—This apron is shown in a different material at figure No. 330 on page 78. In this instance it is made of plaid gingham and trimmed with embroidery. The pattern is in 8 sizes for misses from 8 to 15 years of age, and is suitable for all goods made up into such aprons. For a miss of 13 years, it needs 2¾ yards of material 36 inches wide. Price of pattern, 10d. or 20 cents.

No. 9758.— LADIES' BLANKET WRAPPER.—This wrapper is again shown at figure No. 335 on page 79. A fancy blanket of a heliotrope shade and having a pale pink border was selected in this instance for development. The pattern is in 10 sizes for ladies from 28 to 46 inches, bust measure. For a lady of medium size, it will require 5¼ yards of material 27 inches wide, or 4¾ yards 36 inches wide, or 3¼ yards 48 inches wide. As represented, the garment requires a blanket of twelve-quarter size. Price of pattern, 1s. 3d. or 30 cents.

9758

9758

LADY DOLLS' SET No. 95.—Consisting of a street costume.—This costume is also shown at figure No. 264 on page 63 of this issue. Plain dress goods were employed for the costume in the present instance, with lace for trimming. The Set is in 7 sizes for dolls from 12 to 24 inches in height. To make the costume for a lady doll 22 inches in height, will require 1⅜ yard of material 22 inches wide. Price of Set, 7d. or 15 cents.

9794

9794

No. 9794.—LADIES' WALKING SKIRT.—This skirt is decidedly stylish in appearance. The pattern is in 9 sizes for ladies from 20 to 36 inches, waist measure. To make the garment for a lady of medium size, will require 10⅜ yards of material 22 inches wide, or 5⅞ yards of goods 48 inches wide. Price of pattern, 1s. 3d. or 30 cents.

FIGURE NO. 335.—LADIES' BLANKET WRAPPER.—This illustrates Ladies' wrapper No. 9758, which is also pictured on page 78 of the present issue. In this instance a pale blue blanket was used for the garment, and the Greek-key border is in pale pink. The pattern is in 10 sizes for ladies from 28 to 46 inches, bust measure, and costs 1s. 3d. or 30 cents. To make the garment for a lady of medium size, will require 5¼ yards of material 27 inches wide, or 4¾ yards 36 inches wide, or 3¼ yards 48 inches wide. For the construction of the garment as here illustrated, a blanket of twelve-quarter size will be found sufficient.

9763   **9763**

No. 9763.—Child's Wrap.—This
pattern, also shown at figure No. 332
on page 78, is in 6 sizes for children
from 1 to 6 years of age. For a
child of 4 years, it will require
2¾ yards of material 22 inches wide.
Price of pattern, 7d. or 15 cents.

Figure No. 332.—Child's
Wrap.—This is Child's wrap
No. 9763, again pictured on page
76. The pattern is in 6 sizes for
children from 1 to 6 years of
age, and costs 7d. or 15 cents.
For a child of 4 years, it needs
2¾ yards of material 22 inches
wide, or 1⅜ yard 48 inches wide.

No. 81. — Pattern for a Rag
Doll, published December, 1882.—
Bleached or unbleached muslin, Can-
ton flannel or any material suitable
for a rag doll may be made up by
this pattern. It is in 7 sizes for dolls
from 12 to 24 inches in height. To
make a doll 22 inches tall, requires ¾
yard of goods either 27 or 36 inches
wide. Price of pattern, 7d. or 15 cents.

9759   **9759**

Figure No. 318.—Ladies' Costume.—This illustrates Ladies'
costume No. 9759, which may be seen in two views on page 76.
Plain and all-over embroidered chambray are stylishly combined
in the present instance. The pattern is in 13 sizes for ladies from
28 to 46 inches, bust measure. To make the costume of one
material for a lady of medium size, requires 10½ yards 22 inches
wide, or 6¾ yards 36 inches wide, or 5⅛ yards 48 inches wide.
To make it without trimming, of plain and embroidered
goods 27 inches wide, needs 6 yards of the plain and 2⅝
yards of the embroidered. Price of pattern, 1s. 6d. or 35 cents.

No. 9759.—Ladies' Costume.—This costume is again seen at figure No.
318 on page 75. The pattern is in 13 sizes for ladies from 28 to 46 inches,
bust measure. To make the costume of one material for a lady of medium
size, needs 10½ yards 22 inches wide, or 5¼ yards 48 inches wide. Without
trimming, of plain and embroidered goods 27 inches wide, it needs 6 yards
of plain and 2⅝ yards of embroidered. Price of pattern, 1s. 6d. or 35 cents.

No. 9769.—GIRLS' COSTUME.—This pattern, again shown at figure No. 342 on page 81, is in 10 sizes for girls from 3 to 12 years of age. For a girl of 8 years, it needs 3⅞ yards of chambray and 1 yard of tucked nainsook 27 inches wide, with ½ yard of plain nainsook 36 inches wide. Price of pattern, 10d. or 20 cents.

9769

9769

GIRL DOLLS' SET NO. 50.—Consisting of a Night-Dress and Night-Cap, published January, 1880.—The little garments pictured in these engravings are made of linen, with narrow embroidery as decoration. If a warmer material than linen be desired, flannel, merino or cashmere may be selected, with satisfaction to both the maker and the wearer. The Set is in 7 sizes for dolls from 12 to 24 inches tall. In making the garments for a girl doll 22 inches in height, ⅝ yard of material 36 inches wide will be required. Price of Set, 7d. or 15 cents.

FIGURE NO. 325.—GIRLS' HOUSE COSTUME.—This consists of Girls' dress No. 9764, pictured on page 75; and apron No. 9742, shown on page 78. Both patterns are in 7 sizes for girls from 3 to 9 years of age: the apron costing 7d. or 15 cents; and the dress, 10d. or 20 cents. For a girl of 8 years, they need 3 yards of goods 36 inches wide: the apron needing 1 yard; and the dress, 2 yards.

9742

No. 9742.—GIRLS' APRON.—Another view of this apron is given at figure No. 325 on page 77 of this issue. Nainsook is the material illustrated in the present instance, with embroidery for garniture. The pattern is in 7 sizes for girls from 3 to 9 years of age. For a girl of 8 years, it will require 1 yard of material 36 inches wide. Price of pattern, 7d. or 15 cents.

FIGURE NO. 342.—GIRLS' COSTUME.—This illustrates Girls' costume No. 9769, which is again pictured on page 85 of this issue. The pattern is in 10 sizes for girls from 3 to 12 years of age. To make the costume of one material for a girl of 8 years, will require 6⅓ yards 22 inches wide, or 2⅞ yards 48 inches wide. Price of pattern, 10d. or 20 cents.

No. 9764.—GIRLS' GABRIELLE DRESS.—This pattern, also seen at figures Nos. 323 and 325 on pages 76 and 77, is in 7 sizes for girls from 3 to 9 years old. For a girl of 8 years, it needs 3¼ yards 22 inches wide, or 2 yards 36 inches wide, or 1½ yard 48 inches wide. Price, 10d. or 20 cents.

9764

9764

No. 5.—DOLLS' BODY.—This engraving represents a well-shaped body for a doll, which may be made of any material used for dolls' bodies. The pattern is in 7 sizes for dolls from 12 to 24 inches in height. For a doll 20 inches tall, it needs ⅝ yard of muslin 22 inches wide, with ⅜ yard of kid 5 inches wide for the arms and hands. Price of pattern, 7d. or 15 cents.

5

FIGURE NO. 323.—GIRLS' GABRIELLE DRESS.—This is Girls' dress No. 9764, which is differently represented on page 75. The pattern is in 7 sizes for girls from 3 to 9 years of age. To make the dress for a girl of 8 years, will require 3¼ yards of material 22 inches wide, or 1½ yard 48 inches wide. Price of pattern, 10d. or 20 cents.

No. 9851.—CHILD'S DRESS.—This pattern, again pictured at figure No. 388 on page 90, is in 4 sizes for children from 6 months to 3 years of age. For a child of 2 years, it needs 2⅕ yards of goods 22 inches wide. As shown, it needs ⅝ yard of material 36 inches wide, with 1½ yard of embroidered flouncing 11 inches deep, and ¾ yard of embroidered webbing 20 inches wide. Price, 7d. or 15 cents.

9851

9851

No. 9766.—LADIES' BASQUE.—Another view of this basque is afforded at figure No. 329 on page 78 of this issue. The pattern is in 13 sizes for ladies from 28 to 46 inches, bust measure. To make the basque for a lady of medium size, will require 4⅝ yards of material 22 inches wide, with ⅞ yard of contrasting goods 22 inches wide. Of goods 48 inches wide, 1¾ yard of the one and ⅜ yard of the other will be sufficient. Price of pattern, 1s. or 25 cents.

9766

9766

No. 9765.—LADIES' WALKING SKIRT —This pattern, again seen at figure No. 329 elsewhere on this page, is in 9 sizes for ladies from 20 to 36 inches, waist measure. For a lady of medium size, it requires 12¼ yards of goods 22 inches wide, or 6⅝ yards 48 inches wide. As pictured, it needs 7¾ yards 22 inches wide for the draperies, with 3¼ yards of lining 36 inches wide for the skirt-gores and breadth. Price, 1s.3d.or30cts.

9765

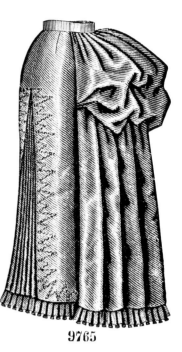

9765

FIGURE NO. 329.—LADIES' TOILETTE.—This consists of Ladies' walking skirt No. 9765, which is shown again elsewhere on this page; and basque No. 9766, also pictured on page 77. The skirt pattern is in 9 sizes for ladies from 20 to 36 inches, waist measure, and costs 1s. 3d. or 30 cents. The basque pattern is in 13 sizes for ladies from 28 to 46 inches, bust measure, and costs 1s. or 25 cents. To make the costume for a lady of medium size, will require 17⅝ yards of material 22 inches wide.

FIGURE NO. 366.—GIRLS' SAILOR COSTUME.—This illustrates Girls' costume No. 9777, again shown on page 86. The pattern is in 8 sizes for girls from 5 to 12 years of age. To make the costume for a girl of 8 years, will require 3¾ yards of material 27 inches wide, together with ½ yard of Silesia 36 inches wide for the waist. Price of pattern, 1s. or 25 cents.

9777   **9777**

No. 9777.—GIRLS' SAILOR COSTUME.—Another illustration of this jaunty costume is given at figure No. 366 on page 85 of this issue. The pattern is in 8 sizes for girls from 5 to 12 years of age. For a girl of 8 years, it requires 3¾ yards of goods 27 inches wide, or 2½ yards 36 inches wide, each with ½ yard of Silesia 36 inches wide, for the waist. Price of pattern, 1s. or 25 cents.

No. 9773.—Misses' Costume.—Another view of this costume is given at figure No. 369 on page 86 of this issue. Flannel was used in this instance, with machine-stitching and buttons as trimming. The pattern is in 8 sizes for misses from 8 to 15 years of age. For a miss of 13 years, it needs 11⅔ yards of goods 22 inches wide, or 5⅞ yards 48 inches wide. Price of pattern, 1s. 3d. or 30 cents.

9773

9773

Figure No. 369.—Misses' Costume.—This illustrates Misses' costume No. 9773, which is pictured in two views, showing a different selection of material, on page 83 of this issue. Light-weight cloth of a navy-blue shade was chosen for the development of the mode in the present instance. The pattern is in 8 sizes for misses from 8 to 15 years of age, and costs 1s. 3d. or 30 cents. For a miss of 13 years, it needs 11⅜ yards of material 22 inches wide, or 6¼ yards 36 inches wide, or 5⅝ yards 48 inches wide.

9770

No. 9770.—Misses' Spanish Girdle.—This pattern, again shown at figure No. 367 on this page, is in 8 sizes for misses from 8 to 15 years of age. For a miss of 13 years, it needs ⅝ yard of material 22 inches wide, with ⅝ yard of silk for lining. Price of pattern, 5d. or 10 cents.

Figure No. 367.—Misses' Costume.—This consists of Misses' costume No. 9771, which is represented in two views on page 84; and girdle No. 9770, again portrayed elsewhere on this page. The costume is here developed in figured sateen of a pink and olive mixture, and the girdle is made of olive velvet. Each pattern is in 8 sizes for misses from 8 to 15 years of age: the girdle costing 5d. or 10 cents; and the costume, 1s. 3d. or 30 cents. For a miss of 13 years, the costume needs 8 yards of material 22 inches wide, or 4⅞ yards 36 inches wide, or 3⅞ yards 48 inches wide; while the girdle needs ⅝ yard of material 22 inches wide, with ⅝ yard of silk for lining.

9771

9771

No. 9771.—Misses' Costume.—Another illustration of this costume, showing it developed in different material, with other trimming, may be observed at figure No. 367 on page 86. The pattern is in 8 sizes for misses from 8 to 15 years of age. To make the costume for a miss of 13 years, will require 8 yards of material 22 inches wide, or 4⅞ yards 36 inches wide, or 3¾ yards 48 inches wide. Price of pattern, 1s. 3d. or 30 cents.

No. 9774.—
MISSES' TUCKED
BLOUSE.—Another view of this
blouse is given at
figure No. 346 on
page 81. The pattern is in 8 sizes
for misses from 8
to 15 years of age.
For a miss of 13
years, it needs $3\frac{7}{8}$
yards 22 inches
wide, or $1\frac{3}{4}$ yard
48 inches wide.
Price of pattern,
10d. or 20 cents.

9774

9774

9799

No. 9799.—LADIES' WRAP.—
Silk, satin, Ottoman, velours and
all seasonable goods may be made
up in this way. The pattern is in 10
sizes for ladies from 28 to 46 inches,
bust measure. For a lady of medium
size, it needs $3\frac{1}{4}$ yards of goods 22
inches wide, or $1\frac{1}{4}$ yard either 48 or
54 inches wide. Price, 1s. or 25 cts.

9586

No. 9586.—MISSES' KILT SKIRT.
—At figure No. 251 on page 61,
this skirt is also shown. The
pattern is in 8 sizes for misses
from 8 to 15 years of age. To
make the garment for a miss of
13 years, requires 7 yards of
material 22 inches wide. Price
of pattern, 1s. or 25 cents.

FIGURE NO. 261.—GIRL DOLLS'
NIGHT-DRESS.—This is the night-dress
in Girl Dolls' Set No. 96, which also includes a chemise and drawers, and is
shown on page 61 of this issue. The
Set is in 7 sizes for dolls from 12 to 24
inches in height, and costs 7d. or 15
cents. For a girl doll 22 inches tall, it
requires $\frac{7}{8}$ yard of goods 36 inches wide.

FIGURE NO. 346.—MISSES' TOILETTE.—This consists of Misses' blouse No. 9774, also shown on page
86; over-skirt No. 9775, again seen on page 84; and
kilt skirt No. 9586, shown on page 64. The three patterns are each in 8 sizes for misses from 8 to 15 years
of age: the blouse and over-skirt each costing 10d. or
20 cents; and the skirt, 1s. or 25 cents. For a miss of
13 years, they need $14\frac{1}{2}$ yards of goods 22 inches wide.

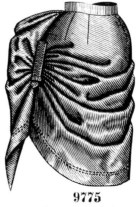

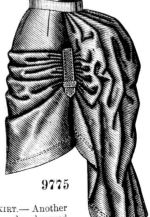

9775

9775

No. 9775.—MISSES' OVER-SKIRT.— Another
illustration of this garment may be observed
at figure No. 346 on page 81. The pattern is
in 8 sizes for misses from 8 to 15 years of age.
To make the garment for a miss of 13 years, will require $3\frac{1}{4}$
yards of material 22 inches wide, or 2 yards 36 inches wide, or
$1\frac{3}{4}$ yard 48 inches wide. Price of pattern, 10d. or 20 cents.

No. 9778.—
MISSES' JACKET.
—Another illus-
tration of this
jacket is given at
figure No. 345 on
page 81. The pat-
tern is in 8 sizes
for misses from 8
to 15 years of age.
For a miss of
13 years, it will re-
quire 3¼ yards of
material 22 inches
wide, or 2¾ yards
27 inches wide, or
1½ yard 48 inches
wide. Price of pat-
tern, 10d. or 20 cts.

9778

9778

9776

FIGURE No. 345. — MISSES' STREET TOILETTE. —
This consists of Misses' jacket No. 9778, again shown
on page 86; and skirt No. 8082, also pictured on page
46. Both patterns are in 8 sizes for misses from 8 to
15 years of age: the jacket costing 10d. or 20 cents;
and the skirt, 1s. or 25 cents. For a miss of 13 years,
they need 7 yards of material 22 inches wide: the
skirt requiring 3¾ yards; and the jacket, 3¼ yards.

No. 9776.—MISSES' POLONAISE.—This pattern,
again shown at figure No. 364 on page 85, is in 8
sizes for misses from 8 to 15 years of age. For a
miss of 13 years, it needs 5⅝ yards 22 inches wide,
or 3⅜ yards 36 inches wide. Price, 1s. or 25 cents.

9776

FIGURE No. 364.—MISSES' POLONAISE COSTUME.
—This consists of Misses' polonaise No. 9776, which
is differently pictured on page 83 of the present publication; and skirt No. 8082, also represented on
page 46. Both patterns are in 8 sizes for misses
from 8 to 15 years of age, and each costs 1s. or 25
cents. To make the costume for a miss of 13 years,
will require 9⅜ yards of material 22 inches wide: the
polonaise needing 5⅝ yards; and the skirt, 3¾ yards.

No. 9779.— GIRLS' COSTUME. — This pattern, again shown at figure No. 363 elsewhere on this page, is in 7 sizes for girls from 3 to 9 years of age. For a girl of 8 years, it needs 4⅜ yards of one material and 2¼ yards of another 22 inches wide. Price, 10d. or 20 cts.

9779

9779

FIGURE No. 363.—GIRLS' COSTUME.—This illustrates Girls' costume No. 9779, which is differently pictured elsewhere on this page. The costume is developed in nun's-vailing and Surah in this instance, lace forming the trimming. The pattern is in 7 sizes for girls from 3 to 9 years of age. To make the costume for a girl of 8 years, will need 4⅜ yards of one material and 2¼ yards of contrasting goods 22 inches wide, or 2¼ yards of the one and 1½ yard of the other 48 inches wide. Price of pattern, 10d. or 20 cts.

No. 9780. —CHILD'S DRESS.— This pattern, also shown at figure No. 357 on page 84, is in 6 sizes for children from 1 to 6 years of age. For a child of 4 years, it needs 4⅝ yards 22 inches wide,

9780

9780

or 3¼ yards 36 inches wide. Price, 7d. or 15 cents.

FIGURE No. 357.—CHILD'S DRESS.—This illustrates Child's dress No. 9780, again shown on page 82. The pattern is in 6 sizes for children from 1 to 6 years of age, and costs 7d. or 15 cents. For a child of 4 years, it needs 4⅝ yards of goods 22 inches wide, or 3¼ yards 36 inches wide, or 2½ yards 48 inches wide.

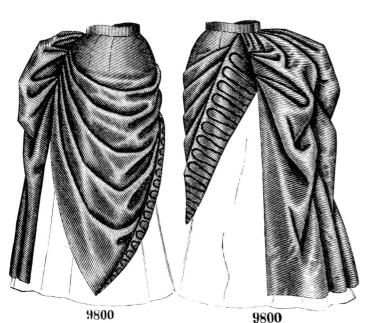

9800

9800

No. 9800.—LADIES' OVER-SKIRT.—Plain dress goods of a medium texture were employed for this stylish over-skirt, and facings of the material and narrow braid form the decorations. The draperies are very deep and full, that of the front being turned up in *lavandière* fashion on the left-side. The back is made very *bouffant* by plaits and loopings. The pattern is in 9 sizes for ladies from 20 to 36 inches, waist measure. For a lady of medium size, it needs 5½ yards of goods 22 inches wide, or 3 yards 48 inches wide. Price of pattern, 1s. or 25 cts.

9804

9804

No. 9804. — LADIES' WALKING SKIRT. — This stylish pattern for a walking skirt is in 9 sizes for ladies from 20 to 36 inches, waist measure. To make the garment for a lady of medium size, will require 6½ yards of plain material and 5 yards of figured goods 22 inches wide, or 3¼ yards of the one and 2½ yards of the other 48 inches wide. Price of pattern, 1s. 3d. or 30 cents.

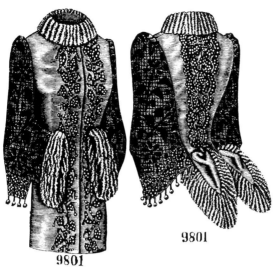

9801

9801

No. 9801.—LADIES' WRAP.—This pattern is in 10 sizes for ladies from 28 to 46 inches, bust measure. For a lady of medium size, it needs 3¾ yards of material 22 inches wide, or 1½ yard 48 inches wide, or 1⅜ yard 54 inches wide. If made of plain and brocaded goods, it requires 2⅝ yards of plain and 1¼ yard of brocaded 22 inches wide. Price of pattern, 1s. or 25 cents.

No. 9781. — LADIES' BASQUE.—This pattern, also seen at figure No. 344 on this page. is in 13 sizes for ladies from 28 to 46 inches, bust measure. For a lady of medium size, it will require 3¼ yards of one material and 1 yard of another 22 inches wide. Price, 1s. or 25 cents.

9781

9781

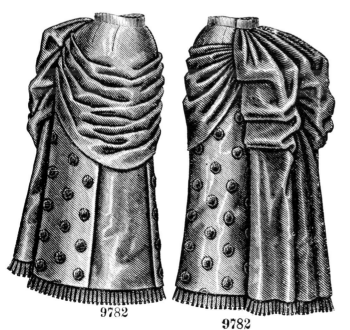

9782

9782

No. 9782.—LADIES' WALKING SKIRT.—This skirt may again be seen at figure No. 344 on page 81. The pattern is in 9 sizes for ladies from 20 to 36 inches, waist measure. For a lady of medium size, it needs 9 yards of plain material and 1½ yard of figured goods 22 inches wide, or 4¾ yards of the one and ⅞ yard of the other 48 inches wide. Price of pattern, 1s. 3d. or 30 cents.

FIGURE NO. 344.—LADIES' TOILETTE.—This consists of Ladies' basque No. 9781, which is differently pictured elsewhere on this page; and skirt No. 9782, represented in two views on page 86. Velvet and camel's-hair are united in this instance, with the materials, fringe and *passementerie* for trimming. The basque pattern is in 13 sizes for ladies from 28 to 46 inches, bust measure, and costs 1s. or 25 cents. The skirt pattern is in 9 sizes for ladies from 20 to 36 inches,-waist measure, and costs 1s. 3d. or 30 cents. To make the toilette of one material for a lady of medium size, will require 15¼ yards 22 inches wide; the basque calling for 4½ yards, and the skirt for 10¾ yards.

FIGURE No. 247.—GIRL DOLLS' COSTUME, published December, 1882. —This is Girl Dolls' Set No. 79, again shown on page 57 of this issue. Dark blue cashmere was used for it in this instance, and embroidery of the same shade is employed for trimming. It is in 7 sizes for dolls from 12 to 24 inches in height, and costs 10d. or 20 cents. For a girl doll 22 inches tall, the dress will require 1 yard of goods 22 inches wide, while the cap will need ¼ yard in the same width.

9809 **9809**

No. 9809.—LADIES' WALKING SKIRT.—These engravings picture a combination of velvet and camel's-hair. The front-draperies are prettily cross-wrinkled by plaits and are quite unique in their arrangement. Medallion ornaments of braid border their loose edges, and a narrow box-plaiting trims the lower edge of the skirt. The pattern is in 9 sizes for ladies from 20 to 36 inches, waist measure, and may be used for one or more fabrics, with any pretty trimmings. For a lady of medium size, it needs 4½ yards of one material and 4⅛ yards of contrasting goods 22 inches wide. Price of pattern, 1s. 3d. or 30 cents

9783 **9783**

FIGURE No. 352.—LADIES' COSTUME.—This illustrates Ladies' costume No. 9783, pictured in a single variety of material, with a different decoration, elsewhere on this page. A combination of plain and fancy novelty suiting is represented in the present instance, with a small quantity of each fabric for decoration. The pattern is in 13 sizes for ladies from 28 to 46 inches, bust measure, and costs 1s. 6d. or 35 cents. To make the costume of one material for a lady of medium size, requires 15¼ yards 22 inches wide, or 7½ yards 48 inches wide.

No. 9783.—LADIES' COSTUME.—This stylish and attractive costume is again represented at figure No. 352 elsewhere on this page. The pattern is in 13 sizes for ladies from 28 to 46 inches, bust measure. To make the costume for a lady of medium size, will require 15¼ yards of material 22 inches wide, or 7½ yards of goods 48 inches wide. Price of pattern, 1s. 6d. or 35 cents.

FIGURE NO. 246.—BABY DOLLS' CHRISTENING ROBE.—This robe is included in Baby Dolls' Set No. 17, which is also shown elsewhere on this page. Fine nainsook is the fabric used for it in this instance, and embroidery forms the decoration. The Set is in 7 sizes for dolls from 12 to 24 inches tall. To make the robe for a baby doll 22 inches high, requires ⅞ yard of material 36 inches wide. Price of Set, 1s. or 25 cents.

No. 9803.—LADIES' BASQUE.—Plain and brocaded dress goods are included in this stylish basque, with buttons for decoration. The pattern is in 13 sizes for ladies from 28 to 46 inches, bust measure. For a lady of medium size, it needs 3 yards of material 22 inches wide, or 1⅜ yard 48 inches wide, with ½ yard of contrasting goods 22 inches wide for the fans and facings. Price of pattern, 1s. or 25 cents.

9803

9803

No. 9807.—LADIES' JACKET. This jacket is made of plain cloth and decorated with silk cord and buttons. The pattern is in 13 sizes for ladies from 28 to 46 inches, bust measure. For a lady of medium size, it needs 3⅞ yards of goods 22 inches wide, or 1¾ yard 48 inches wide. Price of pattern, 1s. or 25 cents.

9807

9807

No. 9784.—LADIES' COSTUME.—Another view of this garment, exhibiting a single material, may be seen at figure No. 355 elsewhere on this page. The pattern is in 13 sizes for ladies from 28 to 46 inches, bust measure. For a lady of medium size, it needs 7¾ yards of plain material and 7¼ yards of figured goods 22 inches wide, or 4⅜ yards of the one and 3½ yards of the other 48 inches wide. Price 1s. 6d. or 35 cents.

9784

9784

FIGURE NO. 355.—LADIES' COSTUME.—This illustrates Ladies' costume No. 9784, which is exhibited in a combination of plain and fancy goods elsewhere on this page. Cheviot suiting was employed in the present instance, with braid for garniture. The pattern is in 13 sizes for ladies from 28 to 46 inches, bust measure, and costs 1s. 6d. or 35 cents. To make the costume for a lady of medium size, will require 15 yards of material 22 inches wide, or 7⅞ yards 48 inches wide.

9786

9786

No. 9786.—
CHILD'S COSTUME.
—This pattern, al-
so seen at figure
No. 348 on page
82, is in 5 sizes
for children from
2 to 6 years of
age. For a child
of 4 years, it
needs $4\frac{1}{8}$ yards 22
inches wide, or $2\frac{5}{8}$
yards 36 inches
wide, or 2 yards
48 inches wide.
Price, 7d. or 15 cts.

FIGURE No. 347.—LADIES' COSTUME.—This illustrates Ladies' costume No. 9785, again shown on this
page. The pattern is in 13 sizes for ladies from
28 to 46 inches, bust measure, and costs 1s. 6d. or
35 cents. For a lady of medium size, it needs $14\frac{7}{8}$
yards 22 inches wide, or $7\frac{1}{2}$ yards 48 inches wide.

FIGURE No. 348.—CHILD'S COS-
TUME.—This illustrates Child's costume No. 9786, again pictured on
page 81. The pattern is in 5 sizes
for children from 2 to 6 years of
age, and costs 7d. or 15 cents. For
a child of 4 years, it requires $4\frac{1}{8}$
yards of material 22 inches wide.

9785

9785

No. 9785.—LADIES' COSTUME.—This costume is also shown at figure No. 347 elsewhere on this page. The pattern
is in 13 sizes for ladies from 28 to 46 inches, bust measure. To make the garment for a lady of medium size,
will require $9\frac{5}{8}$ yards of striped goods and $5\frac{1}{4}$ yards of plain material 22 inches wide. If goods 48 inches wide
be chosen, then $4\frac{3}{4}$ yards of the striped and $2\frac{3}{4}$ yards of the plain will suffice. Price of pattern, 1s. 6d. or 35 cents.

No. 9792.
GIRLS'
JACKET.—
This pat-
tern, also
shown at fig-
ure No. 365
on page 85,
is in 7 sizes
for girls
from 3 to 9
years of age.
For a girl of
8 years, it
needs 2¾
yards 22 inches wide. Price of pattern, 7d. or 15 cents.

9792   **9792**

FIGURE NO. 365.—GIRLS' OUTDOOR TOI-
LETTE.—This consists of Girls' jacket No.
9792, which is again portrayed on page
82 of this publication; and skirt No.
8327, pictured on page 46. Both the jacket and skirt patterns are in 7 sizes for girls
from 3 to 9 years of age: the jacket costing 7d. or 15 cents; and the skirt, 10d. or
20 cents. To make the costume for a girl
of 8 years, will require 4⅝ yards of material 22 inches wide; the jacket calling
for 2¾ yards, and the skirt for 1⅜ yard.

FIGURE NO. 362.—LADIES' BLOUSE COSTUME.—This illustrates
Ladies' costume No. 9790, differently pictured on page 86. Figured nun's-vailing is here shown. The skirt is bordered with a
gathered ruffle of the same set on to form its own heading.
The pattern is in 13 sizes for ladies from 28 to 46 inches,
bust measure, and costs 1s. 6d. or 35 cents. For a lady of medium
size, it needs 16⅓ yards of material 22 inches wide, or 10¾ yards
36 inches wide, or 8¼ yards 48 inches wide, each with 1⅓ yard of
Silesia 36 inches wide for the blouse lining, and ¾ yard of belting.

9790   **9790**

No. 9790.—LADIES' BLOUSE COSTUME.—At figure No. 362 on
page 84, another illustration of this costume is given. The pattern
is in 13 sizes for ladies from 28 to 46 inches, bust measure. To
make the garment for a lady of medium size, requires 16⅓ yards
of material 22 inches wide, or 10¾ yards 36 inches wide, each
with 1⅓ yard of Silesia 36 inches wide, for the blouse lining,
and ¾ yard of belting. Price of pattern, 1s. 6d. or 35 cents.

9793

No. 9793. — CHILD'S JACKET. —This pattern, also shown at figure No. 360 on page 84, is in 6 sizes for children from 1 to 6 years old. For a child of 4 years, it needs 2¼ yards 22 inches wide, or 1 yard 48 inches wide. Price of pattern, 7d. or 15 cents.

9793

FIGURE NO. 360.—CHILD'S JACKET.—This illustrates Child's jacket No. 9793, again pictured on page 82. The pattern is in 6 sizes for children from 1 to 6 years of age, and costs 7d. or 15 cents. For a child of 4 years, it needs 2¼ yards of goods 22 inches wide, or 1⅞ yard 27 inches wide, or 1 yard 48 inches wide.

9795

9886

FIGURE NO. 343.—GIRLS' COSTUME.—This illustrates Girls' costume No. 9795, which is shown again on page 85. The pattern is in 7 sizes for girls from 3 to 9 years of age. Of one material for a girl of 8 years, it needs 4¼ yards 22 inches wide, or 1⅞ yard 48 inches wide, each with 2 yards of ribbon for the sash. Price of pattern, 10d. or 20 cents.

9795

9886

No. 9795.—GIRLS' COS-TUME.—This costume is again shown at figure No. 343 on page 81 of this issue. The pattern is in 7 sizes for girls from 3 to 9 years of age. For a girl of 8 years, it needs 4¼ yards of goods 22 inches wide, or 1⅞ yard 48 inches wide, each with 2 yards of ribbon for the sash. Price of pattern, 10d. or 20 cts.

No. 9886.—CHILD'S DRESS. —A different illustration of this dainty dress may be seen at figure No. 413 on page 96. The pattern is in 6 sizes for children from 1 to 6 years of age. To make the garment for a child of 4 years, will require 2¼ yards of material 22 inches wide, or 1¼ yard 36 inches wide, or 1⅜ yard 48 inches wide. Price of pattern, 10d. or 20 cents.

FIGURE NO. 399.—CHILD'S COSTUME.—This illustrates Child's costume No. 9896, which is again illustrated on page 97 of this issue. The costume is here pictured as made of plain and figured chambray and chambray embroidery, the latter being also used for trimming. The pattern is in 5 sizes for children from 2 to 6 years of age, and is adapted to all dress goods devoted to children's costumes. To make the garment for a child of 4 years, requires 2⅞ yards of material 22 inches wide, or 1⅝ yard 36 inches wide, or 1¼ yard 48 inches wide. Price of pattern, 10d. or 20 cents.

FIGURE NO. 354.—CHILD'S COS-TUME.—This illustrates Child's cos-tume No. 9796, again shown on page 82. The pattern is in 5 sizes for children from 2 to 6 years of age, and costs 7d. or 15 cents. To make the costume for a child of 4 years, needs 4⅛ yards of goods 22 inches wide.

9796

No. 9796. —CHILD'S COSTUME. — This pat-tern, again shown at figure No. 354 on page 83, is in 5 sizes for children from 2 to 6 years old. Of one material for a child of 4 years, it needs 4⅛ yards 22 inches wide. Price, 7d. or 15 cents.

9796

No. 9797.—Ladies' Costume.—Another view of this costume may be seen at figure No. 341 on page 81 of this issue. The pattern is in 13 sizes for ladies from 28 to 46 inches, bust measure, and may be selected for any preferred dress goods. To make the costume for a lady of medium size, requires 13⅝ yards of goods 22 inches wide, or 9¼ yards 36 inches wide, or 7 yards 48 inches wide. Price of pattern, 1s. 6d. or 35 cents.

9797

9797

No. 9709.—Girls' Coat.—This pattern is in 7 sizes for girls from 3 to 9 years of age, and is adapted to all coating fabrics in vogue. For a girl of 8 years, it needs 3 yards of material 22 inches wide, or 2⅜ yards 27 inches wide, or 1½ yard 48 inches wide. Price of pattern, 7d. or 15 cents.

9709

9709

9810

9810

No. 9810.—Ladies' Wrap.—India cashmere was used in the construction of this wrap, with feather bands for trimming. The pattern is in 10 sizes for ladies from 28 to 46 inches, bust measure. To make the garment for a lady of medium size, needs 5 yards of material 22 inches wide, or 2⅕ yards 48 inches wide. If goods 54 inches wide be chosen, 1⅞ yard will suffice. Price of pattern, 1s. or 25 cents.

Figure No. 341.—Ladies' Costume.—This illustrates Ladies' costume No. 9797, which is shown in two views on page 83. The costume is here developed in plain chambray, and the trimming includes the fashionable foot-plaiting of the material and chambray embroidery in two widths. The pattern is in 13 sizes for ladies from 28 to 46 inches, bust measure. To make the costume, without the trimming, for a lady of medium size, will require 13⅝ yards of material 22 inches wide, or 9¼ yards 36 inches wide, or 7 yards 48 inches wide. Price of pattern, 1s. 6d. or 35 cents.

No. 9871.—CHILD'S JACKET.—By referring to figure No. 390 on page 90, this jacket may be again seen. Dark brown coating is the fabric here portrayed, and narrow braid forms the finish. The pattern is in 6 sizes for children from 1 to 6 years of age. For a child of 4 years, it needs 1¾ yard of goods 22 inches wide, or ⅞ yard 48 inches wide. Price of pattern, 7d. or 15 cents.

9871   9871

FIGURE No. 390.—CHILD'S OUT-DOOR TOILETTE.—This consists of Child's jacket No. 9871, also shown on page 91; and slip No. 8665, again seen on page 51. Both patterns are in 6 sizes for children from 1 to 6 years of age: the jacket costing 7d. or 15 cents; and the slip, 10d. or 20 cents. For a child of 4 years, they need 4 yards 22 inches wide.

No. 9819.—LADIES' COLLAR. — This pattern is in one size, and, for a collar like it, will need ⅔ yard of goods either 22 or 48 inches wide. Price of pattern, 5d. or 10 cents.

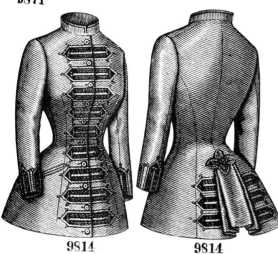

9814   9814

No. 9814.—LADIES' COAT.—Cloth was used for making the coat here pictured, and braid provides the decoration. If desired, facings or machine-stitching may be used as the only finish. The pattern is in 13 sizes for ladies from 28 to 46 inches, bust measure. For a lady of medium size, it will require 4¼ yards of goods 22 inches wide, or 2¼ yards 48 inches wide, or 1¾ yard 54 inches wide. Price of pattern, 1s. 3d. or 30 cents.

9819

9798   9798

No. 9798.—LADIES' POLONAISE.—Another view of this stylishly devised garment may be observed by referring to figure No. 350 on page 82. The pattern is in 13 sizes for ladies from 28 to 46 inches, bust measure, and is adapted to all varieties of dress goods. For a lady of medium size, it will require 7¼ yards of material 22 inches wide, or 5¾ yards 36 inches wide, or 3⅜ yards 48 inches wide. Price of pattern, 1s. 3d. or 30 cents.

FIGURE No. 350.—LADIES' POLONAISE COSTUME.—This consists of Ladies' polonaise No. 9798, which is portrayed in two views on page 85 of this issue; and skirt No. 9275, illustrated again on page 27. The polonaise pattern is in 13 sizes for ladies from 28 to 46 inches, bust measure, and costs 1s. 3d. or 30 cents. The skirt pattern is in 9 sizes for ladies from 20 to 36 inches, waist measure, and costs 1s. 3d. or 30 cents. To make the costume of one material for a lady of medium size, will require 17¼ yards 22 inches wide: the polonaise needing 7¼ yards; and the skirt, 10 yards.

No. 9812. —Child's Street Costume.—This pattern, again seen at fig. No. 361 on page 84, is in 6 sizes for children from 1 to 6 years old. For a child of 4 years, it needs 3¼ yards 22 ins. wide. Price, 10d. or 20 cts.

9812   **9812**

Figure No. 361. — Child's Street Costume.— This illustrates Child's costume No. 9812, again shown on page 81. The pattern is in 6 sizes for children from 1 to 6 years of age. To make the costume for a child of 4 years, will require 3¼ yards of material 22 inches wide. Price of pattern, 10d. or 20 cents.

Figure No. 388.—Child's Dress.— This illustrates Child's dress No. 9851, which is shown again on page 91. The pattern is in 4 sizes for children from 6 months to 3 years of age, and is equally stylish when developed in a combination of materials or a single fabric. For a child of 2 years, it needs 2⅖ yards of goods 22 inches wide, or 1⅛ yard 48 inches wide. Price of pattern, 7d. or 15 cents.

Figure No. 349.—Ladies' Costume.—This illustrates Ladies' costume No. 9802, differently pictured on page 86. The pattern is in 13 sizes for ladies from 28 to 46 inches, bust measure. For a lady of medium size, it requires 13½ yards of material 22 inches wide, or 6⅝ yards 48 inches wide. Price of pattern, 1s. 6d. or 35 cents.

No. 9802.— Ladies' Costume.—A reference to figure No. 349 on page 82 of the present issue, will disclose another view of the handsome costume pictured in these engravings. Figured foulard is the material employed in the present instance, with the same and lace for trimming. The pattern is in 13 sizes for ladies from 28 to 46 inches, bust measure. To make the garment for a lady of medium size, will require 13½ yards of material 22 inches wide, or 7⅞ yards 36 inches wide, or 6⅝ yards 48 inches wide. Price of pattern, 1s. 6d. or 35 cents.

9802   **9802**

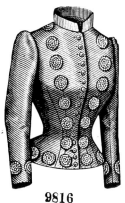

No. 9816.—Ladies' Basque.—This basque is here made of cashmere and trimmed with medallion ornaments of braid. The pattern is in 13 sizes for ladies from 28 to 46 inches, bust measure, and will develop very handsomely in all varieties of dress goods in vogue. For a lady of medium size, it requires 3 yards of material 22 inches wide, or 1¼ yard of goods either 48 or 54 inches wide. Price of pattern, 1s. or 25 cents.

9816

9816

Figure No. 368.—Ladies' Toilette.—This consists of Ladies' walking skirt No. 9805, also shown elsewhere on this page; and basque No. 9806, shown in a different combination of material and trimming on page 85. The pattern to the skirt is in 9 sizes for ladies from 20 to 36 inches, waist measure, and costs 1s. 3d. or 30 cents. The pattern to the basque is in 13 sizes for ladies from 28 to 46 inches, bust measure, and costs 1s. or 25 cents.

No. 9806.—Ladies' Basque.—A different view of this basque is given at figure No. 368 on page 86 of this issue. The pattern is in 13 sizes for ladies from 28 to 46 inches, bust measure. To make the garment for a lady of medium size, will require 3⅞ yards of material 22 inches wide, or 1¾ yard of goods 48 inches wide. Price of pattern, 1s. or 25 cents.

9806

9806

9805

9805

No. 9805.—Ladies' Walking Skirt.—This skirt is differently pictured at figure No. 368 elsewhere on this page. The pattern is in 9 sizes for ladies from 20 to 36 inches, waist measure. To make the garment for a lady of medium size, will require 10 yards of material 22 inches wide, or 5 yards 48 inches wide. Price of pattern, 1s. 3d. or 30 cents.

No. 9838.—CHILD'S COSTUME, WITH ADJUSTABLE COLLAR.—This costume is especially commendable for its simplicity in construction. The pattern is in 5 sizes for children from 2 to 6 years of age. For a child of 4 years, it needs 3¼ yards of goods 22 inches wide, or 1⅝ yard 48 inches wide. Price of pattern, 10d. or 20 cents.

9838

9838

9817   9817

No. 9817.—CHILD'S DRESS.—This pattern, again shown at figure No. 358 on page 84, is in 7 sizes for children from 6 months to 6 years of age. Of one material for a child of 4 years, it requires 2¾ yards 22 inches wide, or 1⅝ yard 48 inches wide. Of plain and embroidered goods, it needs 1½ yard of plain goods 36 inches wide and ½ yard of embroidered webbing 20 ins. wide. Price, 7d. or 15 cts.

FIGURE NO. 358.—CHILD'S DRESS.—This illustrates Child's dress No. 9817, also pictured on page 82. The pattern is in 7 sizes for children from 6 months to 6 years of age, and costs 7d. or 15 cents. For a child of 4 years, it needs 1½ yard of goods 36 inches wide, with ½ yard of embroidered webbing 20 inches wide.

9808   9808

FIGURE NO. 356.—LADIES' COSTUME.—This illustrates Ladies' costume No. 9808, which is portrayed in a combination of plain and figured material, with different decoration, on page 83 of this publication. Surah and novelty suiting are stylishly united in the present instance, with a plaiting of the Surah and silver-tinsel braid as garniture. The pattern is in 13 sizes for ladies from 28 to 46 inches, bust measure, and costs 1s. 6d. or 35 cents. To make the costume of one material for a lady of medium size will require 14⅞ yards 22 inches wide, or 7¼ yards 48 inches wide.

No. 9808.—LADIES' COSTUME.—At figure No. 356 on page 84, another view of this costume is given. The pattern is in 13 sizes for ladies from 28 to 46 inches, bust measure. For a lady of medium size, it needs 12¼ yards of plain material and 2⅔ yards of figured goods 22 inches wide, or 6 yards of the one and 1¼ yard of the other 48 inches wide. Price of pattern, 1s. 6d. or 35 cents.

No. 9818. — GIRLS' APRON. — The pattern to this apron is in 7 sizes for girls from 3 to 9 years of age. To make the garment for a girl of 8 years, requires 2¼ yards of material 36 inches wide, with ¼ yard of tucked material 27 inches wide for the yoke and facing. Price of pattern, 7d. or 15 cents.

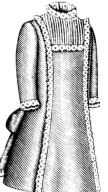

9818   **9818**

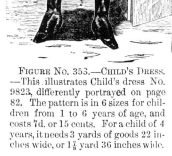

FIGURE No. 353.—CHILD'S DRESS. —This illustrates Child's dress No. 9823, differently portrayed on page 82. The pattern is in 6 sizes for children from 1 to 6 years of age, and costs 7d. or 15 cents. For a child of 4 years, it needs 3 yards of goods 22 inches wide, or 1⅞ yard 36 inches wide.

No. 9823. —CHILD'S DRESS.—This pattern, also seen at figure No. 353 on page 83, is in 6 sizes for children from 1 to 6 years of age. For a child of 4 years, it needs 3 yds. 22 ins. wide, or 1⅞ yard 36 inches wide. Price, 7d. or 15 cents.

9823   **9823**

FIGURE No. 351.—LADIES' COSTUME.—This illustrates Ladies' costume No. 9811, which is shown in two views, each representing different materials, on page 86. The pattern is in 13 sizes for ladies from 28 to 46 inches, bust measure. To make the costume, without the trimming, for a lady of medium size, requires 6¼ yards of goods 22 inches wide, and 3¾ yards of lace net 27 inches wide. Of one material throughout, it needs 10⅞ yards 22 inches wide, or 6⅝ yards 36 inches wide, or 5¼ yards 48 inches wide. Price of pattern, 1s. 6d. or 35 cents.

9811

No. 9811.— LADIES' COSTUME. — This costume may be again seen at figure No. 351 on page 82. The left-hand view shows the adaptability of the mode to dark-colored materials and the right-hand view the effect of light fabrics. The pattern is in 13 sizes for ladies from 28 to 46 inches, bust measure, and may be selected for any desired fabric. To make the garment for a lady of medium size, needs 6⅜ yards of plain material 22 inches wide and 3¾ yards of lace net 27 inches wide. Of one material, it requires 10⅞ yards 22 inches wide, or 5½ yards 48 inches wide. Price of pattern, 1s. 6d. or 35 cents.

9811

9827   **9827**

No. 9827.—Child's Dress.—Other views of this dress may be seen at figures Nos. 385 and 386 on page 90. The pattern is in 6 sizes for children from 1 to 6 years of age. For a child of 4 years, it needs 1⅜ yard of goods 36 inches wide, with ¼ yard of embroidered webbing 20 inches wide. Price of pattern, 7d. or 15 cents.

Figures Nos. 385 and 386.—Child's Dress. —These figures illustrate one pattern, which is No. 9827 and is shown on page 88. Figure No. 385 represents the garment made of colored goods, while figure No. 386 shows the adaptability of the pattern to white goods. The pattern is in 6 sizes for children from 1 to 6 years of age. For a child of 4 years, it requires 1⅞ yard of plain goods 36 inches wide, with ¼ yard of embroidered webbing 20 inches wide. Of one material throughout, it needs 3½ yards 22 inches wide, or 1⅝ yard 48 inches wide. Price of pattern, 7d. or 15 cents.

9824   **9824**

Figure No. 359.—Ladies' Costume.—This illustrates Ladies' costume No. 9824, pictured in a similar combination of material and trimming on page 81. The latter, of course, may be replaced by any other decoration preferred. The pattern is in 13 sizes for ladies from 28 to 46 inches, bust measure, and costs 1s. 6d. or 35 cents. For a lady of medium size, it needs 11⅜ yards of goods 22 inches wide, or 5⅞ yards 48 inches wide.

No. 9824.—Ladies' Costume.—Another view of this garment is given at figure No. 359 on page 84 of this issue. Woolen suiting was employed in this instance, with spangled tinsel braid for decoration. The lower edge of the skirt is trimmed with a double box-plaiting of the material. The body portion is shaped in basque style in front and in polonaise style at the back, and is finely fitted by darts and seams. The pattern is in 13 sizes for ladies from 28 to 46 inches, bust measure. For a lady of medium size, it requires 11⅝ yards of goods 22 inches wide, or 5⅞ yards 48 inches wide. Price of pattern, 1s. 6d. or 35 cents.

GIRL DOLLS' SET NO. 96. — CONSISTING OF A NIGHT-DRESS, CHEMISE AND DRAWERS.—The night-dress in this Set of garments is again shown at figure No. 261 on page 63. The Set is in 7 sizes for dolls from 12 to 24 inches tall, and may be used for muslin or any under-clothing material, with any admired decoration. To make the garments for a girl doll 22 inches in height, requires ⅞ yard of material 36 inches wide. Price of Set, 7d. or 15 cents.

No. 9828.— GIRLS' COSTUME. —This pattern, again shown at figure No. 383 elsewhere on this page, is in 8 sizes for girls from 5 to 12 years of age. For a girl of 8 years, it needs 3¼ yards of dark goods and 2⅜ yards of light material 22 inches wide. Price of pattern, 1s. or 25 cents.

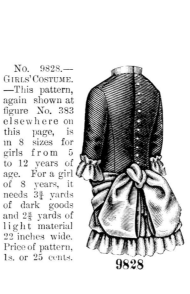

9828   9828

FIGURE NO. 383.—GIRLS COSTUME.—This illustrates Girls' costume No. 9828, which is represented in two views elsewhere on this page. Embroidered nun's-vailing and plain Surah are united in the present instance, and lace provides the trimming. The Surah is draped in sash fashion about the figure and is handsomely bowed at the back. The pattern is in 8 sizes for girls from 5 to 12 years of age, and costs 1s. or 25 cents. To make the costume for a girl of 8 years, will require 3¾ yards of figured goods and 2⅜ yards of plain material 22 inches wide, or 2 yards of the one and 2⅜ yards of the other 48 inches wide.

No. 9830.—MISSES' COSTUME.—At figure No. 393 on page 91, another view of this costume, showing another material, with a different skirt-decoration, may be observed. Nun's-vailing is the fabric illustrated in the present instance, and lace, Surah and silk pompons provide the decorations. The pattern is in 8 sizes for misses from 8 to 15 years of age. To make the garment for a miss of 13 years, will require 7¼ yards of material 22 inches wide, or 4⅞ yards 36 inches wide, or 3⅝ yards 48 inches wide, each with ¾ yard of lining 36 inches wide, and 2 yards of silk 20 inches wide for the sash. Price of pattern, 1s. 3d. or 30 cents.

FIGURE NO. 393.—MISSES' COSTUME.—This illustrates Misses' costume No. 9830, also shown on page 89. Pongee is the material here pictured, with lace and ribbon for garnitures. The skirt is trimmed with a plaiting and scolloped flounces of the pongee and with flounces of deep lace. The pattern is in 8 sizes for misses from 8 to 15 years of age, and costs 1s. 3d. or 30 cents. For a miss of 13 years, it needs 7¼ yards of material 22 inches wide, or 4⅞ yards 36 inches wide, each with ¾ yard of Silesia 36 inches wide, and 2 yards of silk for the sash.

9830   9830

No. 9829.—CHILD'S COSTUME.—This pattern, again shown at figure No. 378 elsewhere on this page, is in 6 sizes for children from 1 to 6 years of age. For a child of 4 years, it needs 3⅝ yards of material 22 inches wide, or 1½ yard 48 inches wide, each with ⅓ yard of Silesia 36 inches wide for the waist. Price, 10d. or 20 cents.

FIGURE NO. 378.—CHILD'S COSTUME. —This illustrates Child's costume No. 9829, also seen elsewhere on this page. The pattern is in 6 sizes for children from 1 to 6 years of age, and costs 10d. or 20 cents. For a child of 4 years, it needs 3⅝ yards 22 inches wide.

FIGURE NO. 380.—LADIES' COSTUME.—This illustrates Ladies' costume No. 9831, which is differently pictured on page 87 of this publication. Plain and figured sateen are combined in the present instance, with very effective results. The costume pattern is in 13 sizes for ladies from 28 to 46 inches, bust measure, and costs 1s. 6d. or 35 cents. To make the garment of one material. for a lady of medium size, will require 12¾ yards 22 inches wide, or 7⅞ yards 36 inches wide, or 6⅝ yards 48 inches wide.

No. 9831.—LADIES' COSTUME.—This stylish costume is portrayed in plain and figured sateen at figure No. 380 on page 89. It is here made of figured foulard, with velvet, lace and ribbon for extraneous garnitures. The skirt is finished with a shirred flounce of the material, which is set on to form a self-heading. The front-drapery is beautifully draped, and is finished at its lower edge with a plaited frill of fine lace. Lace is also applied in *jabot* form down the fronts of the basque and extends in frill fashion along their lower edges. The pattern is in 13 sizes for ladies from 28 to 46 inches, bust measure. For a lady of medium size, it will require 12¾ yards of material 22 inches wide, or 6⅝ yards 48 inches wide. Price of pattern. 1s. 6d. or 35 cents.

No. 9872.—
Girls' Jersey
Basque.—This pattern, again shown
at figure No. 381
on page 89, is in 7
sizes for girls from
3 to 9 years of age.
For a girl of 8
years, it needs 2¼
yards of goods 22
inches wide, or 1
yard 48 ins. wide.
Price of pattern,
7d. or 15 cents.

9872

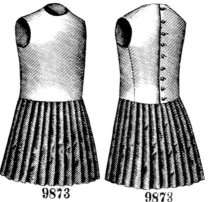

9873   **9873**

No. 9873.—Girls' Kilted Skirt, with
Waist.—This garment is shown made of
frisé suiting and trimmed with velvet at figure No. 381 on page 89. The pattern is in 7
sizes for girls from 3 to 9 years of age. For
a girl of 8 years, it needs 3½ yards of goods
22 inches wide, or 1⅝ yard 48 inches wide,
each with ⅞ yard of lining 36 inches wide
for the waist. Price, 10d. or 20 cents.

Figure No. 381.—Girls' Toilette.—This consists of Girls'
kilted skirt No. 9873, and basque No. 9872, both of which are
shown again on page 88 of the present issue. Each pattern is
in 7 sizes for girls from 3 to 9 years of age: the basque costing
7d. or 15 cents; and the skirt, 10d. or 20 cents. To make the
toilette for a girl of 8 years, will require 5½ yards of goods 22
inches wide: the basque needing 2¼ yards; and the skirt, 3½
yards, together with ⅞ yard of lining 36 inches wide for the
waist. If material 48 inches wide be chosen, then 2⅝ yards
with the quantity of lining goods before mentioned, will suffice.

Figure No. 379.—Ladies' Costume.—This illustrates Ladies' costume No. 9833, two views of which are
given on page 90 of this issue. The pattern is in 13
sizes for ladies from 28 to 46 inches, bust measure,
and costs 1s. 6d. or 35 cents. To make the costume for a lady of medium size, requires 15⅝ yards
of material 22 inches wide, or 7½ yards 48 inches wide.

9833   **9833**

No. 9833.—Ladies' Costume.—Another illustration of this costume is
given at figure No. 379 on page 88 of this publication. Nun's-vailing is developed in the costume in the present instance, and the garnitures include
a knife-plaiting of the material, lace and ribbon. The pattern is in 13 sizes
for ladies from 28 to 46 inches, bust measure. To make the costume for
a lady of medium size, will require 15⅝ yards of material 22 inches wide,
or 7½ yards of goods 48 inches wide. Price of pattern, 1s. 6d. or 35 cents.

9836

No. 9836.—MISSES' JACKET.—This pattern, also seen at figure No. 370 on this page, is in 8 sizes for misses from 8 to 15 years old. For a miss of 13 years, it needs 3½ yards of material 22 inches wide, or 1½ yard 48 inches wide. Price of pattern. 1s. or 25 cts.

9836

9813　　　　**9813**

No. 9813.—LADIES' COAT.—Fancy coating was employed for this stylish garment, with buttons for decoration. The fitting of the garment is superb, and is obtained by means of well curved darts and seams. The fronts are united by buttons and button-holes to some distance below the waist-line, and then flare slightly with a very jaunty effect. The pattern is in 13 sizes for ladies from 28 to 46 inches, bust measure. For a lady of medium size, it will require 4⅝ yards of material 22 inches wide, or 2 yards 48 inches wide, or 1⅝ yard 54 inches wide. Price of pattern, 1s. 3d. or 30 cents.

FIGURE NO. 405.—CHILD'S COSTUME.— This illustrates Child's costume No. 9900, which is portrayed in a different material, with another method of completion, on page 97 of this issue. The pattern is in 5 sizes for children from 2 to 6 years of age, and costs 10d. or 20 cents. To make the garment for a child of 4 years, will require 3⅝ yards of goods 22 inches wide, or 2¼ yards 36 inches wide, or 1½ yard 48 inches wide.

FIGURE NO. 370.—MISSES' TOILETTE.—This consists of Misses' skirt No. 9835, which is also represented on page 89; and jacket No. 9836, again shown elsewhere on this page. Novelty suiting is the material employed for the garment in the present instance, with fancy braid in two widths for trimming. Both patterns are in 8 sizes for misses from 8 to 15 years of age, and each costs 1s. or 25 cents. To make the toilette for a miss of 13 years, will require 10 yards of material 22 inches wide: the skirt needing 6½ yards; and the jacket, 3½ yards. If goods 48 inches wide be selected, then 4⅗ yards will prove sufficient for the purpose; the skirt calling for 3⅜ yards, and the basque for 1¼ yard.

9835　　　　**9835**

No. 9835.—MISSES' WALKING SKIRT.—By referring to figure No. 370 on page 87, another view of this skirt may be observed. The pattern is in 8 sizes for misses from 8 to 15 years of age, and may be employed for a single material or a combination of fabrics. For a miss of 13 years, it needs 6½ yards of goods 22 inches wide, or 3⅜ yards 48 inches wide. Price of pattern, 1s. or 25 cents.

No. 9901.—LADIES' COSTUME.—Another illustration of this handsome costume may be observed at figure No. 396 elsewhere on this page. The pattern is in 13 sizes for ladies from 28 to 46 inches, bust measure, and will be a favorite for tailor-made costumes of cloth, flannel, etc., as well as for chambrays, sateens and similar Summer textures. To make the costume for a lady of medium size, will require 14¼ yards of material 22 inches wide, or 7⅛ yards 48 inches wide. Price of pattern, 1s. 8d. or 40 cents.

9901   9901

9839   9839

FIGURE NO. 377.—LADIES' COSTUME.—This illustrates Ladies' costume No. 9839, which is shown in plain material on page 87. The costume is here represented as made of striped suiting of light texture, and its finish is severely plain. The pattern is in 13 sizes for ladies from 28 to 46 inches, bust measure, and is adapted to all varieties of dress goods at present in vogue. Trimming may be added to the skirt if the plain finish be not liked. For a lady of medium size, it requires 11¾ yards of material 22 inches wide, or 6 yards 48 inches wide. Price of pattern, 1s. 6d. or 35 cents.

No. 9839.—LADIES' COSTUME.—Another illustration of this costume, showing it developed in striped suiting of a light texture, may be observed at figure No. 377 on page 88. The pattern is in 13 sizes for ladies from 28 to 46 inches, bust measure, and may be employed for plain and fancy materials of all varieties. If decoration be desired, it may be added in the form of plaitings or ruffles upon the skirt, while lace, embroidery or braid may be applied to the basque and drapery edges. To make the costume for a lady of medium size, requires 11¾ yards of material 22 inches wide, or 6 yards of goods 48 inches wide. Price of pattern, 1s. 6d. or 35 cents.

No. 9864.—IN-FANTS' BIB.—This little article is here made of piqué and trimmed with nar-row embroidery. It is nicely shaped, and is fastened at the back with a but-ton and button-hole. The pattern is in one size, and, for half a dozen bibs like it, calls for ⅝ yard of material 36 inches wide. Price, 5d. or 10 cents.

9864

9868

No. 9868.—MISSES' FOUR-GORED SKIRT.—The pattern to this well-planned skirt is in 8 sizes for misses from 8 to 15 years of age. For a miss of 13 years, it needs 3¼ yards of goods 22 inches wide, or 1⅝ yard of material either 48 or 54 inches wide. Price of pattern, 10d. or 20 cents.

9815

9815

No. 9815.—LADIES' WRAPPER.—Flowered cash-mere was selected for this garment. The pattern is in 13 sizes for ladies from 28 to 46 inches, bust measure. For a lady of medium size, it will require 9⅝ yards of material 22 inches wide, or 4⅞ yards 48 inches wide. Price of pattern, 1s. 6d. or 35 cents.

No. 9840.—MISSES' COSTUME.—This cos-tume is again shown at figure No. 372 else-where on this page, Plain suiting was em-ployed for its con-struction in this in-stance, and braid, pompons and a hand-some buckle provide the decorations. All varieties of seasonable dress goods are ap-propriate for the de-velopment of the mode, and combina-tions are especially effective. Sequins or tiny buttons may out-line the jacket fronts. The pattern is in 8 sizes for misses from 8 to 15 years of age. For a miss of 13 years, it needs 9⅝ yards of material 22 inches wide, or 4⅞ yards of goods 48 inches wide. Price of pattern, 1s. 3d. or 30 cents.

FIGURE NO. 372.—MISSES' COSTUME.—This illustrates Misses' costume No. 9840, which is shown in a single material, with other decorations, elsewhere on this page. Pongee and brown silk are united in this instance. The skirt is of the pongee and is trimmed with a narrow foot-plaiting of the same. The left side-gore is made of the brown silk and suggests a panel, that is further ornamented by the addition of braid and buttons. Silk is also used for the jacket portions and for the *revers* of the front-drapery. The pattern is in 8 sizes for misses from 8 to 15 years of age, and costs 1s. 3d. or 30 cents. Of one material, for a miss of 13 years, the costume needs 9⅝ yards of goods 22 inches wide, or 4⅞ yards 48 inches wide.

9840

9840

No. 9869. — GIRLS' FOUR-GORED SKIRT.— This pattern is in 7 sizes for girls from 3 to 9 years of age, and is here developed in gray dress goods. For a girl of 8 years, it needs 1½ yard of material 22 inches wide. Price of pattern, 7d. or 15 cents.

9869

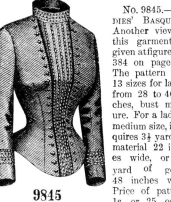

9845

No. 9845.—LA-DIES' BASQUE.— Another view of this garment is given at figure No. 384 on page 89. The pattern is in 13 sizes for ladies from 28 to 46 inches, bust meas-ure. For a lady of medium size, it re-quires 3½ yards of material 22 inch-es wide, or 1½ yard of goods 48 inches wide. Price of pattern, 1s. or 25 cents.

9845

9820

No. 9820. —MISSES' JACKET.— This pattern is in 8 sizes for misses from 8 to 15 years of age. For a miss of 13 years, it requires 3½ yards 22 ins. wide, or 1⅝ yard 48 inches wide. Price, 10d. or 20 cents.

No. 9825.— BOYS' COS-TUME.—This jaunty cos-tume pattern is in 5 sizes for boys from 2 to 6 years of age. To make the costume for a boy of 6 years, needs 3⅝ yards of mate-rial 27 inches wide. Price of pattern, 10d. or 20 cents.

9825   **9825**

9820

FIGURE No. 384.—LADIES' TOILETTE.—This consists of Ladies' basque No. 9845, which is shown again on page 88; over-skirt No. 9843, pictured on page 90; and skirt No. 8645, shown on page 28. The basque pattern is in 13 sizes for ladies from 28 to 46 inches, bust measure, and costs 1s. or 25 cents. The skirt and over-skirt patterns are each in 9 sizes for ladies from 20 to 36 inches, waist measure: the skirt costing 1s. 6d. or 35 cents; and the over-skirt 1s. or 25 cents. In the construction of the toilette for a lady of medium size, 17½ yards of goods 22 inches wide will be required.

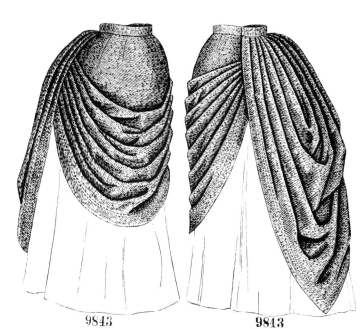

9843   **9843**

No. 9843.—LADIES' OVER-SKIRT.—At figure No. 384 on page 89, this garment is also shown. The engravings picture a novelty in detachable draperies, as over-skirts are often designated. Figured dress goods were employed in this instance, with rows of machine-stitching as a finish. The draping is made by plaits, and the front section falls in deep, oval style. The pattern is in 9 sizes for ladies from 20 to 36 inches, waist measure. For a lady of medium size, it requires 4⅝ yards of material 22 inches wide, or 2⅝ yards 48 inches wide. Price of pattern, 1s. or 25 cents.

No. 9895.—GIRLS' LOW-NECKED DRESS. (TO BE WORN WITH *Guimpe*.)—At figure No. 407 on page 95, this dress is again seen. The pattern is in 10 sizes for girls from 3 to 12 years old. For a girl of 8 years, it needs 3⅜ yards of goods 22 inches wide. Price of pattern, 1s. or 25 cents.

9895   9895

9844

No. 9844.—GIRLS' APRON.—Another view of this dainty little apron is given at figure No. 392 on page 91 of this issue. The pattern is in 7 sizes for girls from 3 to 9 years of age, and may be used for all varieties of washable materials, such as nainsooks, lawns, ginghams, etc. To make the garment for a girl of 8 years, will require 2⅜ yards of material 36 inches wide. Price of pattern, 7d. or 15 cents.

9844

FIGURE NO. 392.—GIRLS' APRON.—This illustrates Girls' apron No. 9844, which is shown in two views on page 90. The apron is here developed in plaid nainsook and trimmed with edging. The pattern is in 7 sizes for girls from 3 to 9 years of age. For a girl of 8 years, it needs 2⅜ yards of goods 36 inches wide. Price of pattern, 7d. or 15 cents.

9847

9847

FIGURE NO. 371.—LADIES' WRAP.—This illustrates Ladies' wrap No. 9847, two views of which, showing it developed in a fine quality of *satin merveilleux*, with lace, *passementerie* ornaments and pompons for decoration, are given elsewhere on this page. The combination of brown Surah silk and beige-colored Spanish lace net is pictured in the present instance, and *beige*-colored lace of the same variety trims it effectively. All wrap materials will develop well by this pattern, and the decorations may be simple or elaborate. The pattern is in 10 sizes for ladies from 28 to 46 inches, bust measure, and costs 1s. or 25 cents. For a lady of medium size it needs 2¾ yards of goods 22 inches wide, or 1¼ yard 48 inches wide.

No. 9847.—LADIES' WRAP.—This wrap is also shown at figure No. 371 elsewhere on this page. It is here made of *satin merveilleux* and handsomely trimmed. The pattern is in 10 sizes for ladies from 28 to 46 inches, bust measure. For a lady of medium size, it will require 2¾ yards of material 22 inches wide, or 1¼ yard 48 inches wide, or 1⅜ yard 54 inches wide. Price of pattern, 1s. or 25 cents.

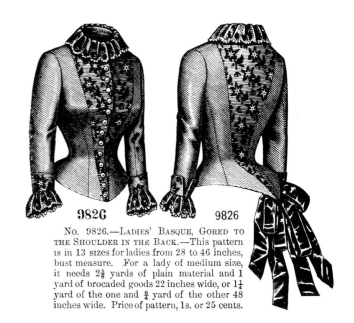

9826   9826

9877

9877

No. 9877.—LADIES' WRAP.—*Satin merveilleux* was employed for this wrap, with lace and *passementerie* for trimming. The pattern is in 10 sizes for ladies from 28 to 46 inches, bust measure. For a lady of medium size, it needs 3¼ yards of material 22 inches wide, or 1⅜ yard 48 inches wide. If 54-inch-wide goods be chosen, then 1¼ yard will suffice. Price, 1s. or 25 cents.

No. 9826.—LADIES' BASQUE, GORED TO THE SHOULDER IN THE BACK.—This pattern is in 13 sizes for ladies from 28 to 46 inches, bust measure. For a lady of medium size, it needs 2⅝ yards of plain material and 1 yard of brocaded goods 22 inches wide, or 1¼ yard of the one and ¾ yard of the other 48 inches wide. Price of pattern, 1s. or 25 cents.

No. 9850.—LADIES' BASQUE.—Another illustration of this basque is given at figure No. 375 on page 88. The pattern is in 13 sizes for ladies from 28 to 46 inches, bust measure. For a lady of medium size, it needs 3¼ yards of one material and 1⅜ yard of contrasting goods 22 inches wide, or 1⅜ yard of the one and ¾ yard of the other 48 inches wide. Price of pattern, 1s. or 25 cents.

9850   9850

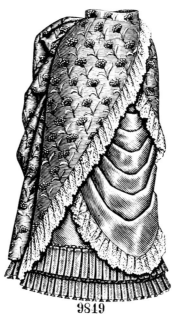

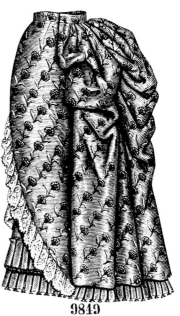

9849   9849

FIGURE NO. 375.—LADIES' TOILETTE.—This consists of Ladies' walking skirt No. 9849, differently illustrated on page 90; and basque No. 9850, also shown on page 90. The skirt pattern is in 9 sizes for ladies from 20 to 36 inches, waist measure, and costs 1s. 3d. or 30 cents. The basque pattern is in 13 sizes for ladies from 28 to 46 inches, bust measure, and costs 1s. or 25 cents. For a lady of medium size, they need 15½ yards 22 inches wide.

No. 9849.—LADIES' WALKING-SKIRT.—At figure No. 375 on page 88 of the present issue, may be observed another illustration of this stylish walking-skirt. Plain and figured foulard are united in this instance, with plaitings of the plain goods and lace for decorations. The pattern is in 9 sizes for ladies from 20 to 36 inches, waist measure. To make the garment for a lady of medium size, will require 6¼ yards of plain material and 4½ yards of figured goods 22 inches wide, or 3¼ yards of the plain and 2⅝ yards of the figured 48 inches wide. Price of pattern, 1s. 3d. or 30 cents.

No. 9822.—GIRLS' POLONAISE.—This pattern is in 7 sizes for girls from 3 to 9 years of age. For a girl of 8 years, it needs 3⅜ yards of material 22 inches wide, or 1⅞ yard either 36 or 48 inches wide. Price of pattern, 10d. or 20 cents.

9822

9822

No. 9857.—LADIES' BASQUE.—This pattern, again shown at figure No. 387 on page 90, is in 13 sizes for ladies from 28 to 46 inches, bust measure. For a lady of medium size, it needs 3¾ yards of goods 22 inches wide, or 1⅝ yard 48 ins. wide. Price of pattern, 1s. or 25 cents.

9857

9857

No. 9858.—LADIES' WALKING SKIRT.—Another illustration of this stylish walking-skirt is given at figure No 387 on page 90 of this publication. Plain dress goods were employed for the skirt in this instance, and a plaiting of the same and tinsel braid form the trimming. The pattern is in 9 sizes for ladies from 20 to 36 inches, waist measure, and is well adapted to either single or combined fabrics. To make the garment for a lady of medium size, will require 11¾ yards of material 22 inches wide, or 5¾ yards of goods 48 inches wide. Price of pattern, 1s. 3d. or 30 cents.

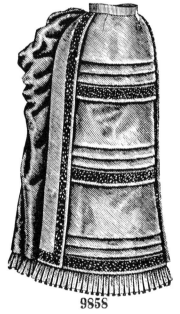

9858

9858

FIGURE No. 387.—LADIES' TOILETTE.—This consists of Ladies' basque No. 9857, also pictured on page 87; and skirt No. 9858, differently portrayed on page 91. The toilette is here represented as made of novelty dress goods, and a plaiting of the material forms the foot finish for the skirt. The basque pattern is in 13 sizes for ladies from 28 to 46 inches, bust measure, and costs 1s. or 25 cents. The skirt pattern is in 9 sizes for ladies from 20 to 36 inches, waist measure, and costs 1s. 3d. or 30 cents. For a lady of medium size, the toilette will require 15¼ yards of material 22 inches wide: the basque needing 3¾ yards; and the skirt, 11¼ yards.

No. 9853.—
Girls' Costume.
—This costume
is again shown
at figure No. 373
on page 87. The
pattern is in 7
sizes for girls
from 3 to 9 years
of age. To make
the garment for
a girl of 8 years,
requires 4⅓ yards
of material 22
inches wide, or
2⅝ yards 36 inch-
es wide, or 2 yds.
48 inches wide.
Price of pattern,
10d. or 20 cents.

9853

9853

No. 9859.—Child's
Dress.—This pattern,
which is again shown
at figure No. 376 on
page 88 of this issue,
is in 6 sizes for chil-
ren from 1 to 6 years
of age. To make the
dress for a child of 4
years, will require 3
yards of goods 22
inches wide, or 1⅝
yard 36 inches wide,
or 1⅜ yard 48 inches
wide. Price of pat-
tern, 7d. or 15 cents.

9859

9859

FIGURE NO. 376.—CHILD'S DRESS.—
This illustrates Child's dress No. 9859,
which is shown in other material on
page 89. The pattern is in 6 sizes for
children from 1 to 6 years of age, and
costs 7d. or 15 cents. For a child of 4
years, it needs 3 yards of goods 22
inches wide, or 1¼ yard 36 inches wide.

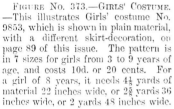

FIGURE NO. 373.—GIRLS' COSTUME.
—This illustrates Girls' costume No.
9853, which is shown in plain material,
with a different skirt-decoration, on
page 89 of this issue. The pattern is
in 7 sizes for girls from 3 to 9 years of
age, and costs 10d. or 20 cents. For
a girl of 8 years, it needs 4¼ yards of
material 22 inches wide, or 2⅝ yards 36
inches wide, or 2 yards 48 inches wide.

No. 9852.—Girls' *Guimpe.*
—This *guimpe* is made of
cambric and lace tucking.
The pattern is in 11 sizes
for girls from 2 to 12 years
of age. For a girl of 8
years, it needs ¾ yard of
cambric 36 inches wide, with
1 yard of lace tucking 27
inches wide for the sleeves,
bands and the upper part
of the *guimpe.* Price of
pattern, 5d. or 10 cents.

9852

9852

No. 9889.—
MISSES'
DRESS.—This
dress is shown
again at figure
No. 406 on
page 95. Wash
goods were
selected for
the dress in
the present
instance, the
material being
tucked for the
yoke. The pat-
tern is in 8
sizes for miss-
es from 8 to
15 years of
age. For a miss
of 13 years, it
needs 6⅝ yards
of material 22
inches wide, or
4 yards 36 in-
ches wide, or
3⅛ yards 48
inches wide.
Price of pat-
tern, 1s. 3d.
or 30 cents.

9889

9889

9821

9821

No. 9821.—MISSES' WALKING SKIRT.—The pattern to the stylish walking-skirt here pictured is in 8 sizes for misses from 8
to 15 years of age, and may be used for any variety of material at present in vogue. To make the garment for a miss of
13 years, will require 9¼ yards of material 22 inches wide,
or 4½ yards 48 inches wide. Price of pattern, 1s. or 25 cents.

No. 9862.

No. 9862.—
Misses' Plain
Waist.—This pat-
tern, also seen at
figure No. 395 on
page 91, is in 8
sizes for misses
from 8 to 15 years
of age. For a miss
of 13 years, it
needs 2⅝ yards of
material 22 inches
wide, or 1⅜ yard
48 inches wide.
Price of pattern,
7d. or 15 cents.

9862

9862

9861

9861

No. 9861.—Misses' Walking Skirt.—This pattern, also shown
at figure No. 395 on page 91, is in 8 sizes for misses from 8 to 15
years of age. For a miss of 13 years, it needs 5¼ yards of plain material and 1⅞ yard of striped goods 22 inches wide, or 2⅞ yards of plain
and ⅞ yard of striped 48 inches wide. Price of pattern, 1s. or 25 cents.

Figure No. 395.—Misses' Toilette.—This consists of
Misses' skirt No. 9861, and waist No. 9862, each shown
again on page 80 of this issue. Both patterns are in 8
sizes for misses from 8 to 15 years of age: the waist costing 7d. or 15 cents; and the skirt, 1s. or 25 cents. To
make the toilette for a miss of 13 years, will require 9¼
yards of material 22 inches wide: the skirt requiring 7⅛
yards; and the waist, 2⅛ yards. If goods 48 inches wide
be selected, then 4⅞ yards will be found sufficient; the
skirt calling for 3¾ yards, and the waist for 1⅛ yard.

No. 9841.—Misses'
Basque.— The pat-
tern to the basque is
in 8 sizes for misses
from 8 to 15 years of
age, and is here deve-
loped in plain dress
goods, with braid for
trimming. For a miss
of 13 years, it requires
3 yards of material 22
inches wide, or 1¼
yard 48 inches wide.
Price of pattern,
10d. or 20 cents.

9841

9841

No. 9837.—
Ladies' House
Dress. — This
shapely dress is
made of reddish-
brown cash-
mere, with a ruf-
fle of the goods,
collar and cuff-
facings of con-
trasting silk, and
ribbon bows for
trimming. Lawn,
sateen, cham-
bray, gingham,
cambric, fine
muslin, cash-
mere or dress
goods of any
suitable texture
will be made up
by this pattern,
with lace, em-
broidery or
braid for the
decorative acces-
sories. The pat-
tern is in 13
sizes for ladies
from 28 to 46 in-
ches, bust meas-
ure. For a lady
of medium size,
it needs 8⅝ yards
of material 22
inches wide, or
5⅜ yards 36 in-
ches wide, or 4¼
yards 48 inches
wide. Price, 1s.
6d. or 35 cents.

9837

9837

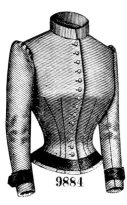

No. 9884.—Ladies' Basque.—At figure No. 416 on page 97, is given another illustration of this basque. Gray suiting of a serge-like variety was the material selected in the present instance, and garnet velvet and crochetted buttons furnish the garnitures. The pattern is in 13 sizes for ladies from 28 to 46 inches, bust measure, and will develop handsomely in serge, cashmere, cloth or any variety of dress goods. For a lady of medium size, it needs 2¾ yards of goods 22 inches wide, or 1¼ yard 48 inches wide. Price of pattern, 1s. 3d. or 5c cents.

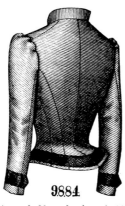

9884

No. 9855.—Ladies' Basque.—This pattern is in 13 sizes for ladies from 28 to 46 inches, bust measure. For a lady of medium size, it requires 3¼ yards of plain material and ⅜ yard of contrasting goods 22 ins. wide. Price, 1s. or 25 cts.

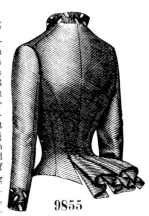

9855

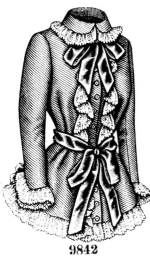

9842

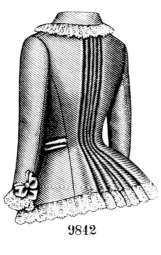

9842

No. 9842.—Ladies' Dressing-Sack.—A different illustration of this dressing-sack is given at figure No. 394 on page 91 of this issue. It is here made of cream-white cashmere and trimmed with oriental lace and satin ribbon. All kinds of white goods, as well as plain and figured wash goods, pongees, silks or Surahs, will be made up in this way, with pleasing results. The pattern is in 13 sizes for ladies from 28 to 46 inches, bust measure. For a lady of medium size, it requires 3¼ yards of material 22 inches wide, or 1⅜ yard 48 inches wide. Price of pattern, 1s. or 25 cents.

Baby Dolls' Set No. 17.—Consisting of a Christening Robe, Gored Dress and Bonnet.—The robe illustrated as forming part of this Set is again shown at figure No. 246 on this page. It is here made of white nainsook, while the dress is of lawn, and the bonnet is of silk. Lace or embroidery may be employed for trimming the bonnet, with handsome effect; or the entire bonnet may be made of embroidered webbing and lined with pale-tinted silk or Surah. The Set is in 7 sizes for dolls from 12 to 24 inches in height. In making the Set for a baby doll 22 inches tall, the robe requires ⅞ yard of muslin 36 inches wide, while the dress needs 1⅜ yard of cambric in the same width, and the bonnet ¼ yard of silk 22 inches wide. Price of Set, 1s. or 25 cents.

Figure No. 394.—Ladies' *Négligé* Toilette.—This consists of Ladies' skirt No. 9867, shown again on page 88; and dressing-sack No. 9842, also seen on page 88. The skirt pattern is in 9 sizes for ladies from 20 to 36 inches, waist measure, and costs 1s. or 25 cents. The dressing-sack pattern is in 13 sizes for ladies from 28 to 46 inches, bust measure, and costs 1s. or 25 cents. For a lady of medium size, they need 8 yards of goods 22 inches wide.

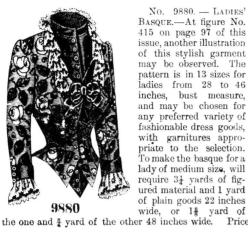

No. 9880. — Ladies' Basque.—At figure No. 415 on page 97 of this issue, another illustration of this stylish garment may be observed. The pattern is in 13 sizes for ladies from 28 to 46 inches, bust measure, and may be chosen for any preferred variety of fashionable dress goods, with garnitures appropriate to the selection. To make the basque for a lady of medium size, will require 3¼ yards of figured material and 1 yard of plain goods 22 inches wide, or 1⅜ yard of

9880

the one and ⅜ yard of the other 48 inches wide.   Price of pattern, 1s. 3d. or 30 cents.

9832

No. 9832.—Ladies' Fancy-Work Apron. — This pretty pattern is in one size, and, to make an apron like it, will require ⅞ yard of material either 22, 36 or 48 inches wide.   Price of pattern, 7d. or 15 cents.

Figure No. 382.—Ladies' Costume.—This illustrates Ladies' costume No. 9870, which is differently pictured on page 90. The pattern is in 13 sizes for ladies from 28 to 46 inches, bust measure. For a lady of medium size, it needs 7¼ yards of plain goods and 10½ yards of figured material 22 inches wide, or 3¼ yards of plain and 5¼ yards of figured 48 inches wide.   Price of pattern, 1s. 6d. or 35 cents.

9846   **9846**

No. 9846.—Ladies' Coat.—Plain cloth was used for this stylish coat, with velvet for the collars, laps and facings. The vest may be of the same material as the facings, or it may be ornamented in any preferred manner. The pattern is in 13 sizes for ladies from 28 to 46 inches, bust measure. For a lady of medium size, it needs 4⅜ yards of material 22 inches wide, or 2 yards 48 inches wide, or 1¾ yard 54 inches wide, each with ⅜ yard of contrasting goods 22 inches wide for the collars, laps, facings, etc.   Price of pattern, 1s. 3d. or 30 cents.

9870   **9870**

No. 9870.—Ladies' Costume.—A different illustration of this costume may be seen by referring to figure No. 382 on page 89 of this issue.   Plain and figured sateen are united in this instance, the arrangement of the two materials being very stylish and effective.   The pattern is in 13 sizes for ladies from 28 to 46 inches, bust measure.   For a lady of medium size, it needs 7¼ yards of plain material and 10½ yards of figured goods 22 inches wide, or 3¼ yards of the one and 5⅜ yards of the other 48 inches wide.   Price of pattern, 1s. 6d. or 35 cts.

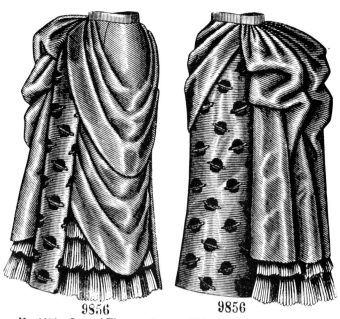

9866

No. 9866.—LADIES' PLASTRON. — This dainty accessory is made of Brussels net and ornamented with Escurial lace edging and jet pendants. The pattern is in one size, and, to make a plastron like it, requires ⅜ yard of material either 20 or 27 inches wide. Price of pattern, 5d. or 10 cents.

9856   **9856**

No. 9856.—LADIES' WALKING SKIRT.—Plain and figured dress goods are combined in this handsomely shaped walking-skirt. Knife-plaitings of the plain goods trim the lower portion of the skirt proper, and upon their sides are arranged panels of the figured goods. The pattern is in 9 sizes for ladies from 20 to 36 inches, waist measure. To make the garment for a lady of medium size, will require 9 yards of plain goods and 2¼ yards of figured material 22 inches wide, or 5 yards of the plain and 1¼ yard of the figured 48 inches wide. Price of pattern, 1s. 3d. or 30 cents.

9897   **9897**

FIGURE NO. 400.—LADIES' COSTUME.—This illustrates Ladies' costume No. 9897, again shown elsewhere on this page. The costume is here shown as made of heavy Surah and Summer Cheviot suiting. The skirt has a knife-plaiting for its foot garniture, and its front-drapery falls in a handsome point almost to the edge at the left side and is draped high on the hip at the right side. The pattern is in 13 sizes for ladies from 28 to 46 inches, bust measure. For a lady of medium size, it needs 11⅞ yards of goods 22 inches wide, or 6 yards 48 inches wide. Price of pattern, 1s. 8d. or 40 cents.

No. 9897.—LADIES' COSTUME.—Figure No. 400 elsewhere on this page, shows this costume developed in a combination of materials, with a different mode of completion. Fancy cloth was selected for its construction in this instance, the material, braid and ribbon forming the garnitures. The pattern is in 13 sizes for ladies from 28 to 46 inches, bust measure. To make the costume for a lady of medium size, will require 11⅞ yards of material 22 inches wide, or 6 yards 48 inches wide. Price of pattern, 1s. 8d. or 40 cents.

9860

9860

No. 9860.—LADIES' WRAP. —Spanish lace net showing a rose pattern was used for this jaunty wrap, and lace edging of a corresponding variety is arranged in *jabot* style about the neck and down each side of the closing, and in a frill about the lower edges.

The pattern is in 10 sizes for ladies from 28 to 46 inches, bust measure. To make the wrap for a lady of medium size, needs 2¼ yards of material 22 inches wide, or ⅞ yard either 48 or 54 inches wide. Price of pattern, 1s. or 25 cents.

9875   **9875**

No. 9875.—CHILD'S COSTUME.—This costume is again shown at figure No. 389 on page 90. The pattern is in 5 sizes for children from 2 to 6 years old. For a child of 4 years, it needs 1½ yard of plain material and 3½ yards of striped 22 inches wide. Price of pattern, 10d. or 20 cents.

9874

No. 9874.—CHILD'S TURKISH CAP.—This jaunty cap is also shown at figure No. 389 elsewhere on this page. The pattern is in 5 sizes for children from 2 to 6 years of age. For a child of 4 years, it needs ½ yard of goods either 22 or 48 inches wide. Price, 5d. or 10 cts.

FIGURE No. 389.—CHILD'S COSTUME.—This consists of Child's costume No. 9875, also seen on page 88; and cap No. 9874, shown elsewhere on this page. Both patterns are in 5 sizes for children from 2 to 6 years of age: the costume costing 10d. or 20 cents; and the cap, 5d. or 10 cents. For a child of 4 years, they need 5½ yards 22 inches wide.

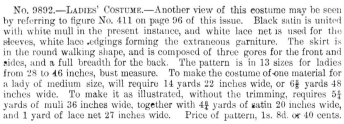

9892   **9892**

No. 9892.—LADIES' COSTUME.—Another view of this costume may be seen by referring to figure No. 411 on page 96 of this issue. Black satin is united with white mull in the present instance, and white lace net is used for the sleeves, white lace edgings forming the extraneous garniture. The skirt is in the round walking shape, and is composed of three gores for the front and sides, and a full breadth for the back. The pattern is in 13 sizes for ladies from 28 to 46 inches, bust measure. To make the costume of one material for a lady of medium size, will require 14 yards 22 inches wide, or 6⅝ yards 48 inches wide. To make it as illustrated, without the trimming, requires 5¾ yards of muli 36 inches wide, together with 4¼ yards of satin 20 inches wide, and 1 yard of lace net 27 inches wide. Price of pattern, 1s. 8d. or 40 cents.

9854   **9854**

No. 9854.—LADIES' WRAPPER.—Striped gingham was used for this comfortable wrapper, and bias bands of the same form the trimming. Cambric, seersucker, calico, cashmere or any other variety of goods may be developed in this way. The pattern is in 13 sizes for ladies from 28 to 46 inches, bust measure. For a lady of medium size, it requires 8¼ yards of material 22 inches wide, or 3¾ yards 48 inches wide. Price of pattern, 1s. 6d. or 25 cents.